CARIBBEAN WARS UNTOLD

CARIBBEAN WARS UNTOLD
A Salute to the British West Indies

Humphrey Metzgen

John Graham

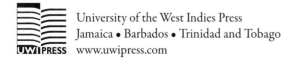

University of the West Indies Press
Jamaica • Barbados • Trinidad and Tobago
www.uwipress.com

University of the West Indies Press
7A Gibraltar Hall Road   Mona
Kingston 7   Jamaica
www.uwipress.com

11 10 09 08 07   5 4 3 2

Metzgen, Humphrey.

Caribbean wars untold: a salute to the British West Indies /
Humphrey Metzgen and John Graham.

p. cm.

Includes bibliographical references.
ISBN: 978-976-640-203-7
1. West Indies, British – History, Military. 2. World War, 1939–1945 –
West Indies, British. I. Graham, John D.C. II. Title.
F1621.M48 2007   940.54'09729

Book and cover design by Robert Kwak.

Set in Sabon and Gill Sans.

Printed in the United States of America.

To all the Caribbean people

Contents

Illustrations

Maps and Charts

Tables

Acknowledgements

This book would not have been possible without the generous cooperation, help and advice we received from numerous bodies: academics, veterans' associations, libraries, museums, military establishments, government departments and High Commissions. We were also very fortunate in securing access to a number of private archives, many of which have never been published before. These sources were found in Barbados, Trinidad, the United Kingdom, Canada, the United States and Germany.

Equally the authors are enormously indebted to a whole host of people from all walks of life. In particular they wish to acknowledge the contributions of Professor Emeritus Woodville Marshall, Dr Glenford Howe and Dr Fitzroy Baptiste of the University of the West Indies, who have dedicated much time and effort to reading the manuscript and suggesting many invaluable improvements.

The authors also wish to acknowledge the work of military historian and researcher Michael Paterson, whose knowledge of and access to many hitherto unknown sources has made the task of writing this book so much easier. A debt of gratitude is owed to Gilly Metzgen, who laboured long hours sub-editing and proof-reading the manuscript.

Finally we wish to thank all those who made contributions, but especially those who sacrificed many hours over the past few years, often at times away from their families, in order that we may pay tribute, by way of this book, to the Caribbean people:

Daphne Agar (Dominica); Warren Alleyne; Michael Bain; Lieutenant-Colonel Leonard Banfield; Claude Bartholomew (Grenada Veterans Association); Carlisle Best (University of the

West Indies Library); Sir Frank Blackman; Ben Bousquet; George Brancker; Herr Horst Bredow (U-Boat Archives, Altenbruch, Germany); George Brizam; Claire Collinson-Jones; Maris Corbin (Barbados); Steve Crossman (British High Commission, Guyana); Derek Davies; Frances Erlinger-Ford (St Lucia); Ira Francis; Lieutenant-Colonel Florence Gittens (Barbados Defence Force); Jill Hamilton; Jollen Harmsen; Dr Edward Harris (Bermuda Maritime Museum); Margaret Harris (journalist/writer, Barbados); Major J.M. Hartland; Michelle Henry (Museum of Antigua and Barbuda); Hugh Hill; Faye Hobson (British High Commission, Trinidad); Cecil Ince; Augustine James; Lieutenant-Commander Gaylord Kelshall (Chaguaramas Military History and Aerospace Museum); Brigadier Rudyard Lewis; Joachim Mark; Julian Marryshow; Douglas Marshall; Christine Matthews (Barbados Department of Archives); Captain Peter Morgan; Kitty Neblett; Desmond Nicholson (Nelson's Dockyard, English Harbour); Dorothy Pilgrim; Jean Pitt (Grenada National Museum); Captain Steven Ramm (Royal Navy); Major Justin Redhead; Owen Rowe; Leonard St Hill; J. St Hill Jones; Captain Peter Short (Council of the Barbados Legion); Frank da Silva; Major-General Joe Singh (Guyana Defence Force); Geoffrey Skeete; Leslie Slater; Sir Frederick Smith; Michael Smith; Linda Speth (University of the West Indies Press); Edward Stoute; Lillian Sylvester (St George's Public Library); William Sylvester; Senator the Honourable Dame Patricia Symmonds; Geoff Tall (Royal Navy Submarine Museum, United Kingdom); Major Peter Tomlin; George Topping; Margaret Walcott (Barbados); Rex Wason; Jodi-Ann Westlake (Bermuda Maritime Museum).

Clearly it is not possible for us to acknowledge everyone by name, because of either the limits of space or a desire to respect anonymity. Equally, even though we have taken every care, any errors or omissions are not those of the contributors but our own.

On matters of intellectual property every effort has been made to trace the copyright holders, but where this has not been possible or where we have inadvertently overlooked our sources, we aim to put the matter right at the earliest opportunity.

Abbreviations

ATS	Auxiliary Territorial Service
BWIR	British West Indies Regiment
CB	Companion of the Order of the Bath
CBE	Commander of the Order of the British Empire
DCM	Distinguished Conduct Medal
DFC	Distinguished Flying Cross
DSO	(Companion of the) Distinguished Service Order
ENSA	Entertainment National Service Association
HMS	His/Her Majesty's Ship
MBE	Member of the Order of the British Empire
MC	Military Cross
MM	Military Medal
NCO	non-commissioned officer
OBE	Officer of the Order of the British Empire
RAF	Royal Air Force
RM	Royal Marines
RN	Royal Navy
U-boat	Unterseeboot (German submarine)
USN	United States Navy
VC	Victoria Cross
WIR	West India Regiment

Introduction

There were two deafening explosions, one a few seconds after the other. They lit up the night with bright orange flames, shattered windows all over town and filled the humid air with the stench of burning fuel. Debris, blown high in the air, clattered down on the concrete quays.

Tied up along the northern wharf of the harbour at Castries in St Lucia were two ships that had arrived in port only that day: 10 March 1942. *Lady Nelson* was a Canadian passenger steamer bound for Barbados. *Umtata* was an eight-thousand-ton British freighter on its way north to join an Atlantic convoy. Now both were burning fiercely as they settled into the harbour mud. Foodstuffs from the steamer's cargo bobbed in the surrounding water, and already local people had jumped in to salvage (or loot) what they could.

The ships had been torpedoed. A German U-boat had worked its way inside the port – a harbour not considered deep or wide enough to need full-scale defences – and had taken aim at the fattest targets. Before they were hit the two vessels had even been lit up. Supplies for the island's American garrison were being unloaded that night and the quayside had been as brightly illuminated as if it were peacetime. Thankfully a third ship, a highly inflammable oil tanker, had its lights off and had not been seen.

Before the American troops could react the attackers were on their way back to the open sea. U-161, which had been unable to submerge because of the shallow water, had sailed past the coastal lookouts, lined up its targets and fired two torpedoes before making its escape on the surface. As it ran back through the channel, a single machine-gun opened fire. A stream of bullets stabbed into the darkness, but the raiders were already gone.

St Lucia was not the only island to suffer this rude awakening. A month earlier the same submarine, U-161, had sunk two tankers off the coast of Trinidad, while four other U-boats had attacked an oil refinery and shipping off the coast of Venezuela. As Samuel Eliot Morison, an exasperated American naval officer, remarked, "U-boats showed the utmost insolence in the Caribbean, their happy hunting-ground."

To the Germans this sea was the "Golden West". The region provided more targets than they could aim at, and a minimum of effective retaliation. There were slow-moving tankers, numerous single vessels and shore bases that were thinly defended by inexperienced troops. U-boats enjoyed such good hunting that they left the area only when their fuel or ammunition ran out. The heavy tonnage of shipping they sank meant that the Caribbean, far from being a backwater in the Second World War, became for a time the most dangerous stretch of sea in the world.

This was because of its strategic importance. Though the West Indian islands were four thousand miles from the land war in Europe, they sat astride a sea lane that led from the Atlantic to the Pacific through the Panama Canal, thus linking both theatres of war. They protected the busy American ports along the Gulf of Mexico and, more significantly, controlled the traffic between Britain and its most important sources of oil, which came from Venezuela via the refineries of Aruba, Curaçao and Trinidad. In addition the islands provided vital supplies of sugar and bauxite, the latter needed for manufacturing aeroplanes.

These things made the region an obvious target. In February 1942 Germany began a major submarine campaign, code-named Operation *Neuland*, aimed at crippling the two most important facilities in the Caribbean: the oil-processing plants on the Dutch islands and the great shipping centre in Trinidad's Gulf of Paria. The first two weeks of Operation *Neuland* achieved remarkable success for the Germans: twelve tankers sunk, five damaged and an oil refinery and other cargo ships damaged. Moreover it had imposed temporary shipping paralysis in the waters off the South American coast. War had come to the West Indies with stealth and with violence.

Throughout its history the Caribbean has alternated between extremes of war and peace, wealth and poverty, tension and repose. For centuries it had been a place of explosive violence as Amerindians, Spaniards, Frenchmen, Dutchmen, Englishmen – and pirates of many nations – fought for control of its resources. For a time its islands were among the wealthiest places on Earth, and the quarrels of far-off Europe were played out in its straits and bays and islands. But its importance dwindled, turmoil ceased and the tide of events flowed elsewhere. It was during this time that "West Indian" became the term that described those who lived in the islands of the Greater and Lesser Antilles – black, white and coloured.

For half a century after the defeat of Napoleon and the abolition of slavery, some of the Caribbean economies, such as Barbados, British Guiana and Trinidad, performed well, but by 1880 the West Indies had become a depressed backwater. However, history had not yet finished with the region. Long after the guns of its forts and fleets had fallen silent, another war brought a new enemy into the western seas, which became as dangerous to sail as they had been in the days of Morgan or Piet Heyn. Ships, laden no longer with silver but with even more valuable cargoes of oil or bauxite, ran the gauntlet of a new form of piracy: the German submarine.

This book examines the conflicts that have shaped the people and places of the West Indies, bringing trade, settlement, conquest, re-conquest, rebellion – a host of influences that created the island-nations and the remaining dependencies of today. In particular, however, it tells the story of the region's role in the World War of 1939 to 1945.

Though thousands of miles removed from the scenes of significant fighting, the Caribbean was now in the front line. Some of its islands were on Hitler's side. Its people suffered attack and experienced loss and destruction. Its resources proved vital to the war effort and its people contributed in a multitude of ways – often in spite of official indifference or obstruction – to the eventual Allied victory, whether as children collecting scrap metal or as crews flying with the Royal Air Force (RAF). Situated at the gateway between the European and Pacific wars, the Caribbean's strategic importance gave rise to a massive American military presence that significantly altered the character and culture of both the islands and the mainland countries that make up the region.

These communities, and their peoples, themselves had an impact on the wider world that was often small but nevertheless significant, on places as disparate as Scotland, Gibraltar, the Crimea and West Africa. The authors describe the West Indies' contribution to Britain, in a tradition of service forged by the militias as far back as the seventeenth century. Much of this story is little-known, and much of it is surprising. We hope that this story will bring a sense of justified pride to those who live in the Caribbean, and that it will stimulate the interest of those who are drawn by curiosity or by pleasure-seeking to this beautiful region.

PART I

Five Hundred Years of International Conflicts and Wars

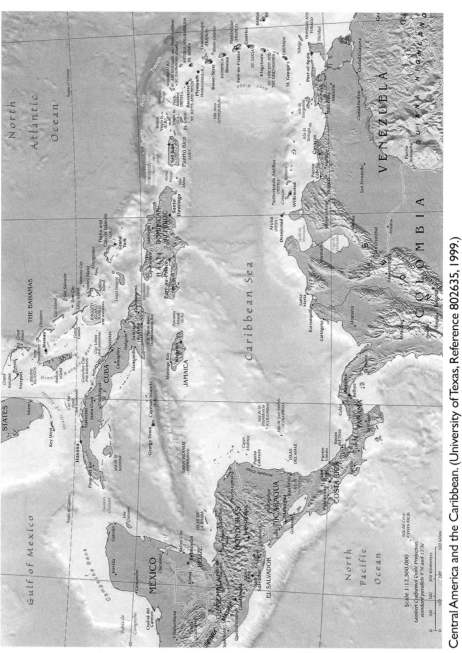

Central America and the Caribbean. (University of Texas, Reference 802635, 1999.)

CHAPTER I
Historical and Conceptual Perspectives

Discoveries, rivalries and settlements.

From a distance the island looked lush, green and inviting. The pleasant scent of tropical vegetation wafted out to sea on the warm air and the treetops were filled with birdsong. From the rail of the *Santa Maria*, Christopher Columbus looked towards a landscape of forest and mountains that was as rich and exotic as he had hoped. He was later to write: "This land is . . . the best that words can describe. It is very high, yet the top of the highest mountain could be ploughed with bullocks, and all is diversified with plains and valleys. In all Castile there is no land that can be compared with this for beauty and fertility."[1]

Somewhere beyond these mountains was the court of the Great Khan, the semi-mythical place that another Italian explorer, Marco Polo, had reached after an epic overland journey more than two hundred years earlier. Now Columbus had found an easier route to the Orient. He had proved that Earth was round and that the East could be reached by sailing west. The island ahead of him, and the many others that dotted the blue-green waters, were, he declared, off the coast of Japan, or perhaps China.

The wealth of Cathay had been the talk of Europe for two centuries. Hugely profitable trade would follow this discovery, though the expedition was also interested in finding gold. Columbus had little doubt that it would be there, in the mountains and rivers of this unfamiliar land. He would return to Europe rich and triumphant. The crews of his three ships – *Nina*, *Pinta* and *Santa*

Maria – were as delighted as their commander. Lacking Columbus's belief in the possibility of reaching the Indies, for them the voyage had been a frightening ordeal. Now they had survived the journey. They would not, after all, perish from thirst or starvation on the seas.

Columbus earned the considerable rewards that he expected to receive. Thought to be the son of a Genoese weaver, at the time of this voyage he was forty-one years old and a capable and experienced mariner. He was also a visionary, a romantic and something of a crank, and his oddness did nothing to instil confidence. He dressed eccentrically, used curious navigational instruments and claimed to hear celestial voices. He had previously crossed the North Atlantic as far as Iceland and was convinced that the ocean had a western shore; for several years he had energetically petitioned the rulers of Europe's maritime powers for patronage and funding. Added to the implausibility of his claims was the problem that his terms were decidedly steep: he expected the title of admiral, the viceroyalty of any territories discovered and a tenth of whatever gold, gems or spices were found.

Columbus approached the King of Portugal, the greatest seafaring nation of the time (the Portuguese Bartholomew Díaz had recently followed the coast of Africa as far as the Indian Ocean) but was rebuffed. The city-states of Venice and his native Genoa declined as, initially, did the Spanish monarchs Ferdinand and Isabella. He wrote to the King of England, Henry VII, and eventually received an invitation to visit his court and explain his scheme in greater detail. This response, however, came too late. In 1492 the Spanish Crown relented and agreed to bear the cost of the expedition. Had the Tudor monarch become Columbus's patron, the history of the Caribbean would have developed very differently, and the whole of Central and South America might have been English speaking – an intriguing concept.

The risk was deemed worthwhile. Trade between Europe and China brought both luxuries and necessities – silks and spices – to the West. They came either by land, a long and often dangerous trade route that was controlled by the Turks, or by sea via a lengthy voyage around the tip of Africa. If a shorter route

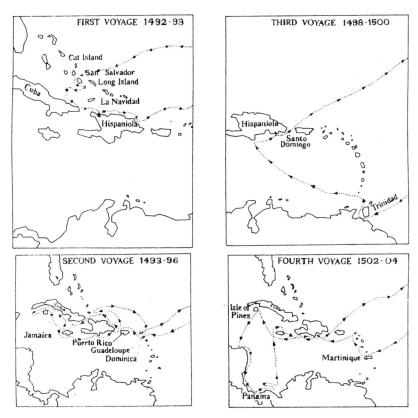

Columbus's four voyages to the Caribbean. (Lennox Honychurch, *The Caribbean People*, vol. 2 [London: Thomas Nelson and Sons, 1980].)

to the Indies could be found, Spain would become the major conduit of trade and gain vast wealth. Ferdinand and Isabella were therefore willing to equip the vessels. Even so, there was a distinct shortage of men willing to serve on them. Though able captains were procured, the crews were assembled largely of criminals from local prisons, who were guaranteed a pardon. Three ships, with ninety men aboard, set sail from the Spanish port of Palos on 3 August 1492. A month later, as they passed the Canary Islands, they left the known world behind and entered seas hitherto crossed solely by legendary Vikings, Celts and West Africans, and never, until the advent of Columbus, by such a large and well-chronicled expedition.

For a further month they lost contact with the world. Then, on 6 October, they sighted flocks of birds to the west. Despite this good omen, the crews demanded to turn back, and only with difficulty did Columbus keep them on their course. He was swiftly vindicated. Barely a day later he saw what appeared to be a light ahead, and the next day, as dawn was breaking, a lookout, Rodrigo de Triana, sighted land (Columbus had offered a silk doublet to the first man to do so). Within a few hours the explorers were ashore, and Columbus planted in the sand the standard of Ferdinand and Isabella, claiming the land for them and Spain.

For the rest of his life (he died in 1506) Columbus believed he had reached the Indies. Though the name would ever afterwards be applied to both the region and its inhabitants, he had actually discovered an entirely different and unknown continent – his expedition had reached the Bahamas. The first landing was on a minuscule islet they named San Salvador. They then spent nine days exploring similar isles and sandbanks before discovering a much larger territory: Cuba. At the beginning of December they found another large and fertile island, which Columbus named Hispaniola, or "Spanish island" – the second-largest island in the Antilles after Cuba. Today two-thirds of the island forms the Dominican Republic and Haiti occupies the rest. It was off this land mass that Columbus breathed in the scent of flowers and imagined himself in the Orient.

Columbus's landfall had been almost exactly in the centre of the New World, halfway between North and South America. His ships had left the Atlantic for a smaller body of water, now called the Caribbean, strung with fertile islands. These formed a two-thousand-mile chain that separated the wider ocean from what was almost an inland sea. Columbus of course knew little of this; only on subsequent voyages would the extent of the region become apparent. The New World was not uninhabited, and from the very first the expedition encountered natives whom they naturally referred to as Indians. There were no khans or mandarins, but Columbus had found a civilization, albeit one that was unrecognizable to Europeans.

The first people to make the region their home had arrived around 2000 BC from what is now Florida. Their name – the

Siboney – is the only thing known about them, for they left behind no artefacts, cultivation or language. About two millennia later another people, the Arawaks, travelled north from the South American mainland along the eastward sweep of the islands, driven by persecution. The Caribs, a fierce rival tribe after whom the Caribbean is named, also originated in South America. They too moved through the great chain of islands in search of land, displacing the Arawaks, who fled before them to settle in new territories until those in turn were overrun. Both native peoples travelled by canoe. They had considerable skill in building and operating these craft, which were large enough for a crew of forty or fifty. The Caribs did not reach every island; when the Spaniards arrived they found members of both tribes. Indeed, Caribs survived in small numbers throughout the subsequent centuries.

The Arawaks were among the gentlest races known to history. They had little crime, serious social inequality, religious dissension or hardship. They had adequate land and the means to live without great effort. The men fished or hunted birds, while the women cultivated crops. They grew maize, cotton, sweet potatoes, cassava and tobacco. It was their staple diet – cassava bread – that gave Arawaks their name "meal eaters". They also drank beer brewed from this plant.

They lived in villages – collections of round huts with wooden beams and a thatched roof of palm leaves. Each community had a headman called a *cacique*, who had a larger hut and a wooden throne but otherwise lived like everyone else. Physically Arawaks were brown-skinned and shorter than Europeans but were graceful and "perfectly made". Their most noticeable characteristic was their forehead. From birth, children had their foreheads flattened by tightly tied boards. The result was the growth of a bone shield so strong that it could withstand a blow from a native weapon, and possibly a European sword.

These were the "Indians" whom Columbus believed to be natives of the Orient. Already persecuted by the Caribs, the Arawaks would not long survive the arrival of the Spaniards. Enslaved, murdered and killed by smallpox, in less than a decade their population was virtually eradicated. Within a century they were gone, though their descendants can be found today in Guyana, Venezuela, the Dominican Republic and parts of Cuba. Although Spain's relations with the native peoples were later to be characterized by greed and violence, during Columbus's time there was peace. Columbus spent the rest of the year 1492 in Hispaniola, where in December he established a settlement called La Navidad, in honour of Christ's birth. In January he set out for Spain, leaving forty of his men to trade with the natives, and landed back at Palos on 15 March 1493.

Columbus's return from the other side of the world caused a sensation, as did his descriptions of what he had found: more islands than had ever been seen in any ocean, and these teeming with plants, flowers and trees previously unknown. There was fertile land for agriculture and the promise of mineral wealth. The success of the expedition changed everything. Spain was to establish not just a monopoly of trade with the Indies but an overseas empire. The route to the East was now open to anyone with the enterprise to make the journey. As well as traders and prospectors, there would be clergy to bring Christianity to the natives.

Columbus's second voyage was very different from his first. He set off on 25 September 1493 with a fleet of seventeen ships that contained fifteen hundred men. There were soldiers, priests, craftsmen and farmers as well as horses, pigs and chickens. The previous time, the Spaniards had come to look. This time they were coming to stay.

The fleet did not follow the same route, and thus made numerous further discoveries. These included the islands of Guadeloupe, Montserrat, Antigua, Nevis, St Croix, St Thomas, St John and Puerto Rico. Reaching Hispaniola and La Navidad, Columbus found the settlement burned and his men killed. In his absence the high-handed behaviour of the Spaniards had provoked a local *cacique* into attacking the town, and everything had been destroyed. This incident marked the end of good relations between the two cultures. Henceforth the size and armament of the Spanish force meant that they were no longer dependent for safety on the natives' goodwill. They could now dominate those with whom they came in contact.

The greatest cause of friction was gold. This undoubtedly existed in the Indies, for Columbus had brought a small amount back from his first voyage. It could be found in Cuba, Hispaniola and Puerto Rico, but deposits were small and they would be exhausted by the 1520s. The natives, when interrogated, always implied that it came from other territories to the south or west. Following their directions, Columbus discovered yet another island – Jamaica – but gold was as elusive there as elsewhere.

Meanwhile another attempt to found a town, this time called Isabella, failed because an unhealthy location was chosen. Despite this, the Spanish colonists settled and began to appropriate land. Although the Indians were supposed to be converted to Christianity and European standards of behaviour, in practice they were quickly enslaved and exploited. They showed no enthusiasm for work or worship and displayed no gratitude for the efforts supposedly being made on their behalf. The attachment of some Indians to cannibalism also alienated them from the Spaniards. Once they had ceased to be deemed worthy of salvation or consideration, their race was doomed by cruelty and diseases to swift extinction.

Spain's discoveries had aroused interest – and envy – throughout Europe, and other nations began to take notice of the Western Hemisphere. To forestall any meddling by these interlopers, Pope Alexander VI was persuaded in 1493 to declare the outer regions of the known world the exclusive property of Spain and Portugal, the latter also an ambitious Catholic imperialist nation with settlements in Africa and Brazil. To prevent a clash of interests between the two nations, the Pope set a line of demarcation from pole to pole, one hundred leagues (three hundred miles) west of the Cape Verde Islands. Portugal was to keep to the east of this line as its vessels travelled round the Cape of Good Hope to India, while Spain was to have exclusive rights to the territories west of it.

The arrangement proved unsatisfactory because Portuguese ships were not left with sufficient room to sail round the west coast of Africa. A final agreement was therefore made between both powers in June 1494, at Tordesillas in northern Spain. The

The papal line of the Treaty of Tordesillas. (James Carnegie and Patricia Patterson, *The People Who Came*, vol. 2 [Edinburgh: Pearson Educational, 1989].)

line was redrawn at 370 leagues west, enabling Portugal to claim Brazil. The Treaty of Tordesillas, backed by papal authority, gave Spain the right to regard any foreign vessels in Caribbean waters as trespassers and pirates. Simple greed, however, quickly led other nations to ignore it. Spain reacted viciously towards any outsiders who were captured, thus beginning a cycle of rivalry and violence that would dominate the region for more than three centuries.

Columbus made two more journeys to the Indies. In 1498, sailing south of his customary route in an attempt to find the source of gold, he discovered the island of Trinidad and the continent of South America. In 1502 he found Martinique and Honduras, Nicaragua and Panama on the Central American mainland. By this time, however, the admiral was no longer a hero. His failure to find either the Great Khan or sufficient gold had lost him favour in Spain. Aging and racked with arthritis, he was making one last attempt to save his credibility. His ships, however, fell foul of a Caribbean plague: shipworms. These riddled the wooden hulls of the three vessels so that they could not re-cross the Atlantic, or even reach Hispaniola. Limping to Jamaica, they were stranded there for eleven months before rescue came – an ignominious end to the career of history's most renowned explorer. He died in obscurity on 20 May 1506.

The life and death of Columbus are more of an enigma than we are perhaps used to imagining. Though he is celebrated in Genoa as a native son, and though Seville honours him with an impressive monument, neither of these may be appropriate. Recent research has suggested that he was not Italian but a Catalonian, born not in Genoa but in Barcelona (here too a memorial commemorates him). It is also plausibly suggested that his remains, though they have supposedly twice crossed the Atlantic, have remained in the New World.

Columbus was initially buried in the church attached to a friary in Valladolid, Spain, where he died. Sometime during the next few years his body was removed to a Carthusian monastery in Seville, but in the mid-1530s his grandson Luis asked the king for permission to re-inter it in the cathedral at Santo Domingo, in Hispaniola. In the following decade Columbus's body was placed in a vault beneath the cathedral with that of his son Diego, and Luis was later also buried there. The remains were undisturbed until 1795, when Spain ceded the whole island to France. It seemed fitting that Columbus's bones should remain on Spanish soil, so they were transferred to the cathedral in Havana.

Almost exactly a century later, in 1899, Cuba became independent. Spanish sovereignty ended on 31 December 1899, though the surrender of Spanish troops had taken place in August, and Spain lost its last foothold in the Western Hemisphere. The coffin containing Columbus was brought back to Seville aboard a naval vessel, and his bones were reburied in the cathedral there. But the story did not end there, for already (in 1877) a vault had been discovered in Santo Domingo next to the one from which he had been exhumed, and the inscription on the coffin read: "The Illustrious and Excellent Man Christopher Columbus". The remains within were examined by an American expert in 1960. His conclusion was that the bones were from two different men – probably Columbus and Diego – and that they had probably been mixed up when disturbed in 1795. Another academic has offered the suggestion that a lead pellet found with the bones could have been the projectile that caused the admiral's gunshot wound (mentioned in one of his letters) during his fourth voyage – a colourful detail, but an unproven theory.[2] DNA tests have cast doubt on the authenticity of the bones in Spain, so might Columbus after all have remained in the lands he discovered?

CHAPTER 2
The Spanish Empire

Spain strengthens its foothold in the New World against the French, English and Dutch privateers who are equally attracted to the riches of the region.

The Spanish conquest was quickly followed by the arrival of increasing numbers of Spaniards who came to the islands to settle, to build and to search for gold. The climate, however, proved an effective enemy. It sapped the health and energy of Europeans and made sustained work impossible. Towns were often sited in unhealthy locations, causing the death rate to soar. The city of Sevilla la Nueva in Jamaica, laid out in 1509 as the island's capital, was so badly situated that in more than twenty-five years only ten children born there survived. The Indians, of course, had less difficulty with the climate, and they were soon pressed into slave labour, but deaths from ill-treatment reduced their numbers so rapidly that within a decade there were not enough to sustain the colonies.

The solution was to import workers from other tropical regions: Amerindians seized from the eastern islands and Africans, who since the 1440s had been sent as slaves to Spain and Portugal. In the first years of the sixteenth century, Africans – termed "Negroes" from the Spanish word for black – were sent to Hispaniola to work in the diggings during the island's gold rush. By the 1520s there was a steady flow of Africans across the Atlantic, and in two decades the supply of indigenous Indian labour had been exhausted and Africans comprised the entire slave populace. The group that was to grow into the largest element of the Caribbean region's population had arrived.

As colonization moved westward onto the South American mainland, the islands declined significantly in importance. The conquest of Mexico by Cortez (1519–21) and of Peru by Pizarro (1531–32) shifted Spanish attention and resources to other regions that promised much greater rewards in terms of wealth. By mid-century the great native American civilizations had been destroyed and their treasure was being shipped back to Spain. The islands were no longer a destination but a way-station. But they were not without value. Settlers had introduced livestock and foodstuffs that gave them an important role in supplying the fleets and armies that passed through. The crops that have dominated Caribbean agriculture ever since – sugar cane, ginger, oranges, lemons, limes and bananas – began to be cultivated during this period. Forests were cleared to reveal fertile farmland and cattle were raised on a large scale to provide beef and hides. Jamaica, which bred goats as well as cattle, became famous for the toughness of its leather, and tanning became an important local industry.

The riches extracted from the South American interior were brought to the coast by slave labour and mule-train. They were shipped from Nombre de Dios, on the isthmus of Panama, or from ports on the "Spanish Main" (the coasts of present-day Colombia and Venezuela) where the great treasure fleets assembled every summer. Their route through the Caribbean was protected by strategic ports and fortifications, though once out in the Atlantic the ships were vulnerable to attack. Spain now had far more land in the region than its settlers needed or could exploit. Though territories of commercial, military or political importance – Cuba, Puerto Rico, Hispaniola (Santo Domingo on this island was the capital of the Spanish Indies) – continued to flourish as colonies, numerous other islands were lost to Spain through surrender or inertia, including Guadeloupe, Martinique, Grenada, Jamaica and even the western part of Hispaniola (now Haiti). The island of Barbados, later to become a source of vast wealth for England, was not even claimed by the Spanish, because to them it had no strategic value.

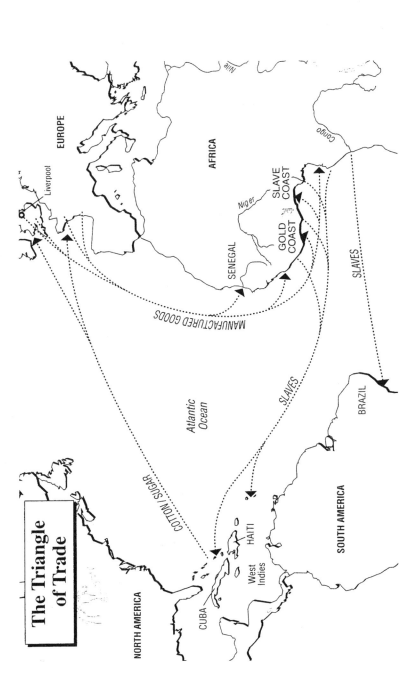

The triangle of trade. (Joseph Kleinman and Eileen Kurtis-Kleinman, *Life on an African Slave Ship* [San Diego: Lucent Books, 2000].)

Piracy

Within a few decades of the Spanish discoveries, the ships of its rivals found and plied the route to the Indies. The first to trespass in Spanish waters were the French, who carried out acts of robbery with increasing frequency. Complacent in their sole possession of the region, the Spaniards had not maintained defences that could resist European gunnery, and they began to pay for this as their ships and ports were seized or destroyed with relative impunity. France and Spain were at war intermittently during the sixteenth century, though French privateers (privately owned armed vessels commissioned for war service by the government) offered no such excuse for their depredations.

When hostilities officially resumed in 1552, the Caribbean felt for the first time the impact of full-scale European warfare. Now the privateers appeared not as single vessels but in whole squadrons, the French flag on their mastheads and their decks crowded with soldiers. Forces of this size did not confine themselves merely to raiding shipping. They besieged, ransomed, sacked and burned coastal cities throughout the Caribbean, including Cartagena on the mainland, La Yaguana in Hispaniola, and Santiago and Havana in Cuba. Frenchmen even attempted to colonize Florida in order to control the vital Florida Channel, through which the treasure fleets came. The venture failed, but Spain was sufficiently unnerved to hastily build fortifications.

Spain was at that time the world's greatest military power and had by far the largest empire. It was also – thanks to the flow of gold and silver from South America – the richest nation. These attacks on its remote and inadequately defended colonial outposts were its first defeats, the first cracks in the façade of Spanish invincibility. But there would soon be others. The Reformation – the religious upheaval that began in Germany in 1517 and continued until the 1560s – divided Europe into two hostile camps, the Catholic south and the Protestant north. Many of the privateers were manned by Huguenots, French Lutherans who were motivated as much by religious animosity as by greed or national interest. The two Protestant emerging maritime nations, England and Holland, also became Spain's religious opponents as well as its commercial rivals, and neither was likely to have any qualms about attacking Spanish interests or possessions.

The crews that sailed the Caribbean in search of booty were not, strictly speaking, pirates. That term referred to a type of sea-robber who acted on his own initiative, was responsible to no one and made no distinction between war and peacetime. Similarly, "buccaneer" was a specific term for those who preyed only on the Spanish. Privateers were vessels, and by extension those who sailed in them. "Corsair" had the same meaning. Corsairs or privateers were equipped and sent overseas by a government or a consortium of merchants to attack the shipping or harbours of other nations, and their backers divided the booty they brought back. Even major expeditions could be privately financed this way; the fleet that raided Puerto Rico in 1598 and sacked the city of San Juan was paid for by the Earl of Cumberland in England.

For the Spanish, French and Dutch rivals, it was the English who became the greatest threat to their commercial, political and military interests. The English had first appeared as early as 1527, when Henry VIII sent Captain John Rut to the West Indies to assess the opportunities for plunder. In the 1560s a sea captain from Devon, John Hawkins, made a series of voyages from West Africa carrying cargoes of slaves, which he sold illegally in Hispaniola. Hawkins, however, carried out no piracy. His ships were nevertheless damaged by the Spaniards and his voyages did not make enough profit to be worth continuing. One of his comrades, Francis Drake, revisited the region in 1570 and looted Panama. Having tasted blood, as it were, Drake returned three years later and captured a whole treasure fleet at Nombre de Dios. This success became a legend – one of the landmarks of privateering in the Caribbean – and encouraged further encroachments. The Indies became synonymous with greed, pillage and violence. England came to surpass France in the scale of destruction that its sailors visited on Spanish ships and cargoes, especially after the defeat of the Armada in 1588. All this enabled Elizabeth I's subjects to see themselves as the premier maritime nation.

Privateers swarmed so thickly in the waters of the Caribbean that a Spanish official wrote in 1568:

> For every two ships that come hither from Spain, twenty corsairs appear. Not a town on this coast is safe, for whenever they please to do so they take and plunder these settlements. Daily we see them seize ships, both those of the Indies trade and also some that come from Spain itself. They capture towns, and this so commonly that we see it happen every year.[1]

The West Indies were Spain's Achilles heel. Remote, sprawling and impossible to defend effectively, they became a hunting ground for any country with a grudge against the Spaniards. The vast wealth that was housed in the ports or transported from the region provided a temptation too great to ignore. By capturing Spain's treasure, its enemies could directly affect its ability to pay for war in Europe.

There were also many Dutch privateers. These men were not, strictly speaking, foreigners, for Holland (the Netherlands, or the Low Countries) was Spanish territory, an outpost of Spain governed from Madrid through a viceroy. In 1572, however, the seven northern provinces rebelled against Spanish rule. The fighting was bitter and Spanish repression brutal but unsuccessful. In 1579 the seven broke away to form a republic, the United Provinces. The war did not end decisively, dwindling into stalemate and truce (Spain did not officially admit defeat until 1643). Nevertheless, it proved a major humiliation for the Spanish empire. The new Dutch nation was small but enterprising, reliant on commercial acumen rather than military prowess. It possessed some of the world's most skilful seamen and shipbuilders as well as merchants of legendary shrewdness. Dutch fleets, searching the world for wealth, were at home in any ocean. Dutch sailors knew, as the French did, that the most effective way to hurt their enemy was to destroy Spain's wealth by sinking or capturing its treasure ships at their source, in the Caribbean, on the Atlantic or in European waters.

Piracy and privateering were to remain characteristic of the West Indies for another century and a half, but another source of wealth – trade – was to overtake mere robbery as the driving force of the region.

CHAPTER 3
Strife and Settlement

Spain continues to dominate the Caribbean but is beginning to lose some of its territories. The economic wealth of the region shifts from gold and silver to sugar.

In the seventeenth century a new pattern became apparent in the Caribbean. While it remained a Spanish sea, the interlopers had clearly come to stay. Spain's rivals sought not just to raid and rob – though those things continued to happen – but also to establish their own permanent colonies. The first to do so were the Dutch, who settled on St Eustatius in 1600. Early English attempts to take St Lucia (1605) and Grenada (1609) were thwarted by local Indians, but they persevered. The English took St Christopher (St Kitts) in 1624, Nevis the following year, Barbados in 1627, Antigua and Montserrat in 1632 and the Bahamas in 1649. France occupied Guadeloupe in 1634 and Martinique and part of the mainland (French Guiana) in 1635. The English already had territories there, and one of the staple crops of the Western Hemisphere – tobacco – was already being cultivated. The early outposts were founded and built in the teeth of ferocious opposition. Though the Spanish did not want every island in the region, they were not willing to see these territories occupied by "heretics" and "pirates", and if they did not raid foreign settlements to destroy crops and dwellings, the local Indians were likely to do so. Once the Thirty Years' War (1618–48) began in Europe, however, Spain became preoccupied with threats nearer home.

Between 1609 and 1621 the war between Spain and the Dutch was in abeyance, the twelve-year truce in itself an admission of Spain's inability to defeat its enemy. Its grip on the Caribbean was weakening, a fact that was most clearly demonstrated in 1627, when a Dutch force commanded by Piet Heyn captured an entire treasure fleet off the coast of Cuba. And though there were fortunes to be made from plunder, the Dutch were interested in other commodities too. Off the mainland of present-day Venezuela (the name means Little Venice) was an immense salt field at Punta Araya. Though deep within Spanish territory, it was constantly visited by ships from Holland to load supplies, as salted herring was a large and important national industry.

The Dutch also discovered another source of wealth: sugar cane. While occupying part of Brazil during the middle decades of the century, the Dutch learned from the Portuguese the secrets of raising cane and extracting juice from the stalks. The full potential of this product would not be achieved for several decades, but the Caribbean had discovered a more constant source of wealth than South American gold and silver. In 1640 sugar cane was introduced to an English island, Barbados. Within ten years it was to become a vastly lucrative export, its cultivation spreading to other islands, and by the following century it had turned the West Indian territories into some of the most profitable real estate on earth.

Sugar and Slaves

Planting and tending crops was done by slaves, but not all the slaves were black. The European colonies also made extensive use of indentured labourers of European origin. These men and women were enticed to the Caribbean by promises of land and wealth or – more frequently – were simply press-ganged. The authorities might also empty the jails to help populate this remote region. Indentured workers served a fixed period, four years in the English colonies and three in the French, while felons served eight. They were treated in every way like slaves and could, for instance, be bought and sold among different planters. Unused to the climate, they were less robust than blacks (three of them were considered worth one African) and were often treated worse. The owner, after all, had his slaves for life, but he had only a few years in which to get as much work as possible out of a European labourer.

If the indentured workers were not criminals, they were often prisoners of war, and for a century and a half the islands were to receive a continuous supply of men who had supported doomed enterprises. Once the English Civil War – to some extent a war of religion between Protestants and Catholics – had begun in 1642,

Hoeing cane

Planting sugar cane

Interior of a boiling house

A millyard

Shipping hogsheads

The five stages of sugar production. (James Carnegie and Patricia Patterson, *The People Who Came*, vol. 2 [Edinburgh: Pearson Educational, 1989].)

Scottish and Irish prisoners of both faiths came in their hundreds. After the Protestant monarchy was restored in the 1660s, this first batch of prisoners was joined decades later by defeated followers of Catholic King James II (and, later still, of the Young Pretender), who tried to replace Protestant with Catholic rule.

As the gulf widened between king and Parliament, royalist sentiment grew stronger in the islands; this became especially noticeable in Barbados, which had its own legislative assembly. Initially there was no serious animosity between local supporters of the two factions, but after the execution of Charles I on 30 January 1649, the situation worsened with the arrival of exiled royalists from England. Through their wealth and influence they made the island into a royalist stronghold and banished parliamentary sympathizers.

The government in London could not ignore such impudence, even in such distant territories (Virginia and the islands of Antigua and Bermuda displayed a similar attitude). Trade with Barbados was banned and a naval force was sent to blockade it. The royalists prepared to fight, but when the ships appeared there was little they could do. The attackers were powerful enough to land their men with confidence, destroying fortifications and taking prisoners. After lengthy negotiations the defenders eventually capitulated, on generous terms.

The Stuart cause seemed lost, but only a year later a royalist fleet appeared in the Caribbean under Prince Rupert of the Rhine. A highly successful cavalry officer, he belonged to an era in which military commanders were expected to serve with equal skill on land and at sea. However, he was too late to rally the king's supporters in the islands and found no glory in these waters. His troops made landings in some colonies, to no great effect, but a hurricane battered his ships and his brother was among many who drowned. A memoir found among Prince Rupert's papers describes their voyage through the islands. The ships engaged in no great sea fights; instead they found their enemies largely in heavily defended forts or harbours. Rupert's forces were unable to do more than annoy them, though they exchanged shots on a number of occasions and took some prizes.

Prince Rupert and his men were received with courtesy by the French, with whom their paths crossed:

We stood for Montserrat, inhabited by the English, where we arrived the next day, being Whitsunday, 1652. We sailed to windward of it, and came about the north point, where standing into the old road, and finding no ships, we bore up to Nevis; We anchored there till night to man our prizes, and prevent them from knowing our course; but his Highness [Prince Maurice, Rupert's brother] finding one of the ships to belong to one of the King's friends, restored both ship and goods. Night being come, we stood for Nevis. The Admiral [Prince Rupert], leaving the rest of the fleet astern a league for fear of discovery, fell in by break of day with Pelican Point. We sailed into the usual road, where were great store of ships, who, having made the whole fleet, began to shift for themselves, some endeavouring to escape by sailing, others by running to shore. His Highness laid the fairest aboard, being close under the fort; which endeavoured her security, but in vain; for being entered, we straight brought her with our shot, and with our pinnace fetched off another that was hauling ashore. They spent divers shot both from fort and ship, but we lost but one man, which was his Highness' secretary, being killed close to him. Their ships were fast aground, so as we could get no prizes off. They exchanged shots freely, and seeing no good could be done, we steered for St Christopher's.

Being fair up Stone's Point, the fort, having advanced the English flag, began to play us hard. His Highness luffing close to it, received their shot, and returning them his, passed into the road the whole fleet during the night. But the Prince perceiving theirs to be hauled close to the shore, and their cables chained, knew nothing more was to be done there, for fear of being becalmed, the land lying very high, and they close under it, so as we must expose our masts to the malice of the fort guns. These considerations kept us from going further, but passing by them we exchanged broadsides, and so came to an anchor in Sandy Point Road, on the French ground, where his Highness was kindly received by their forts and visited by their officers.[1]

Shortly afterwards, England – now a "commonwealth" – declared war on Spain. The Lord Protector, Oliver Cromwell, was convinced that the Spanish were now too weak to defend their Caribbean possessions. He decided that lands could be annexed without difficulty, a scheme that came to be known as the "Western Design". The forces sent to carry this out under Admiral William Penn and Colonel Venables – a fleet and troops from England, assisted by units of local volunteers and militia – were of poor quality. They were soundly defeated in Hispaniola and had to abandon any notion of capturing Cuba. The only island that seemed to offer any prospect of success was Jamaica, which was known to be sparsely populated and inadequately defended. The expedition landed there in May 1655 and seized it on behalf of the Lord Protector. Though the English took possession of the island without great difficulty, a number of Spaniards fled into the interior, where they could easily hide amid mountains and forest. There they joined forces with escaped slaves, known as Maroons, to wage a continuing guerrilla war.

Jamaica would later become a valuable British possession, but at the time the acquisition of this relatively unimportant Spanish territory was seen as no more than a face-saving gesture, undertaken so that the force did not have to return empty-handed. The humiliation was, however, offset somewhat when, two years later, Admiral Blake repeated Piet Heyn's accomplishment and captured an entire treasure fleet off Cadiz – a far more grievous blow to Spain than the loss of Jamaica.

The Dutch, a vigorous seafaring nation, were also England's enemy during this period. During the second of the three wars fought between the two nations during the seventeenth century, ships of the great Admiral de Ruyter fired on Barbados for an entire day. Answered in kind by shore defences, they withdrew without landing.

The restoration of the monarchy brought tranquillity to England but not to the Caribbean, where piracy – and the squabbles of the European nations – continued uninterrupted. The French, once again at war with England, seized Montserrat, Nevis and Suriname and plundered Antigua (making use of vicious Carib allies) with such ferocity that the damage took many years to repair. And while the nations waged war, a parallel, more informal conflict was being carried out by privateers. They captured several Dutch islands, sacked cities in Florida and Central America, and held to ransom the wealthy town of Porto Bello in Panama. One of the privateers, a Welshman named Henry Morgan, became perhaps the most feared figure in Caribbean history; he was later knighted and appointed lieutenant-governor of Jamaica. Not all land transfers were the result of seizure, however. In 1667 England gave the mainland colony of Suriname to the Dutch in exchange for an island thousands of miles to the north: New Amsterdam, which was shortly afterwards renamed New York.

England's "glorious revolution" of 1688 – the deposing of the Catholic James II in favour of the Protestant Dutchman William of Orange – brought war yet again when France sided with James. In the Caribbean, Irish settlers, who naturally supported the Catholic monarch, caused a good deal of trouble to Protestants and their plantations. On St Kitts, which had a number of Irish settlers,

Life on a slave ship. (Joseph Kleinman and Eileen Kurtis-Kleinman, *Life on an African Slave Ship* [San Diego: Lucent Books, 2000].)

France lent its support and took the opportunity of capturing the English part of the island. However, they lost it again only two years later. They also made a determined but unsuccessful attempt to capture Jamaica. This war ended in 1697, but peace was always a relative concept amid the tangled web of rivalries and alliances that governed the West Indies.

Other powers attempted at this time to gain a foothold in the lucrative slave and sugar trades by establishing bases in the region. The Danes arrived on the island of St Thomas in 1672, and shortly afterwards allowed representatives of the Electorate of Brandenburg (later Prussia) to trade there. Sweden founded a

An eighteenth-century drawing of a slave ship. (James Carnegie and Patricia Patterson, *The People Who Came*, vol. 2 [Edinburgh: Pearson Educational, 1989].)

short-lived colony. Even Scotland, though technically part of the United Kingdom along with England, established its own settlement at Darien, on the isthmus of Panama, in 1699, though disease, attacks by neighbouring Spaniards and the hostility of the English caused it to fail almost at once. More important, in 1697 Spain ceded to France the western part of Hispaniola; this wealthy colony, known as Saint-Domingue, gained independence in 1804, taking the name Haiti.

Piracy remained such a problem that for a time there was international cooperation in suppressing it. Foremost among the concerns was trade, particularly the cultivation and export of sugar cane. Sugar had become so important by the 1720s that nothing could be allowed to interfere with its safe transport across the Atlantic. Naval expeditions were sent from England to hunt down pirate vessels in the countless creeks and bays of the islands. They did so effectively, though the most decisive blow in this campaign was struck by nature: in June 1692 an earthquake at Port Royal, Jamaica, swallowed whole a city that had become notorious throughout the world for its concentration of brigands and the ill-gotten wealth within its walls. Despite this, plenty of pirates were left, and it took another thirty years of sustained action (such as mass hangings) before the majority became persuaded that the region was too dangerous. They left for other, less heavily policed oceans.

CHAPTER 4

The Growth of British Power and the Demise of Spain

The superpowers of Spain, Britain and France continue to fight for territories in the Caribbean at a time of wars in Europe (and later America) resulting in Britain gaining new settlements.

The eighteenth century opened with another major European conflict. The War of the Spanish Succession (1701–14) was caused by the threat that a French prince would inherit the throne of Spain, thus greatly expanding the power and influence of Louis XIV. The contest was decided entirely in Europe, where John Churchill, Duke of Marlborough, won a number of major victories that ended the prospect of French military domination (although France effectively won the war by keeping its candidate on the Spanish throne). In the Caribbean there was the usual pattern of tit-for-tat warfare, capture, ransom and counter-attack. The French took Nevis and Britain got the French part of St Kitts. British ships, commanded by Admiral Benbow, made a half-hearted attack on a French squadron, thus letting slip an opportunity for easy victory.

The war lasted until 1713, and the treaty that ended it gave British merchants the right to send one ship a year, loaded with merchandise, to trade in Spanish territory. This was an important concession, even though clandestine trade had flourished in the region since the earliest years. During the fighting on Nevis a good deal of kudos had been earned by the black slaves of English planters, who fought courageously while their masters

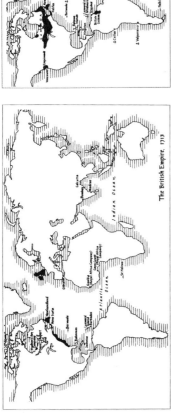

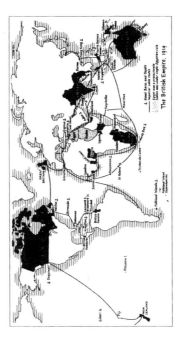

The British Empire in 1713, 1850 and 1914. (Lawrence James, *The Rise and Fall of the British Empire* [London: Little, Brown, 1994].)

were guilty of panic and cowardice. Memories of this service, which was to be repeated in other conflicts throughout the century, influenced the decision to form black regiments in the Caribbean nine decades later.

No sooner was the war over than another grievance surfaced. Since the middle of the seventeenth century, English mariners and loggers had established themselves in Yucatán to cut and ship the valuable wood that grew in the area. Mahogany came from Central America, as did logwood, a commodity that was used in the dyeing of wool, which was England's most significant export. The presence of these communities, whose members also engaged in piracy, was a thorn in the side of the Spanish, who responded with persecution. The loggers' settlements were destroyed altogether in 1716 and they moved north to the banks of the Belize River, where, when Spanish mistreatment continued, the British government protested and allowed reprisals to be carried out.

Spain had been steadily losing power and prestige in the region, but was still capable of bellicose gestures. The most famous of these brought about the "War of Jenkins' Ear". Though Spain had granted limited trading rights in the Caribbean to France and Britain, its authorities continued to vigorously harass their shipping and traders. In 1731 Spaniards boarded a vessel captained by Robert Jenkins, cut off his ear and told him to present it to the King of England as evidence of the fate that awaited trespassers. Eight years later he produced it in the House of Commons; in an atmosphere of mounting anger over Spanish outrages, it proved the final insult, leading to a war that was to last until 1748. Whatever the emotional impact of Jenkins's ear, the anger was fuelled by Spain's continuing insistence on the right to search British ships at sea. The majority of incidents had taken place in the Western Hemisphere, so hostilities were pursued in the West Indies. A naval force commanded by Admiral Vernon sailed to the isthmus of Panama, where it captured Porto Bello. This victory made Vernon a hero in Britain and, intriguingly, he won the favour of the local Spaniards too – by sparing their city the looting and merciless destruction that were usual in Caribbean conflicts.

France became an ally of Spain. In the West Indies, where privateering was continuous, any incident could be used as a pretext for opening hostilities. The conduct of wars also tended to follow a well-worn procedure: islands would be seized and occupied, only to be handed back to their owners in the subsequent peace settlement. In 1744 the French attempted to capture the small island of Anguilla with six hundred men. They met with spirited resistance from a force of one hundred militiamen and, withdrawing, lost their colours, a triumph of which Anguillians have remained proud ever since.

In the midst of this period of strife Britain found itself involved in an internal war in Jamaica – what would nowadays be termed a "police action" – against the Maroons, the descendants of runaway African slaves. This group had spent several generations living in the inaccessible interior of the island, and were adept at living off the land, raiding farms and plantations and evading capture. The army, the Royal Navy and local militia troops spent seven years attempting to suppress the Maroons. Eventually a treaty was signed with their chiefs, guaranteeing that the Maroons would be left in peace provided they ceased to attack plantations and that they handed over runaway slaves.

Despite the frequency with which war came to the West Indies, the slave trade and the sugar trade continued to flourish. Those who owned plantations made such colossal personal fortunes from the latter that it became synonymous with ostentatious wealth. Sugar was as important in the eighteenth century as oil was to become in the twentieth, and possession of – or access to – a source of the commodity became an overriding international preoccupation. Planters from these islands used their wealth to buy property, influence and parliamentary seats in Britain, where they created a formidable political lobby (the "West India Interest"). The price of West Indian sugar was kept prohibitively high, despite public outrage. Such tenacity proved self-defeating, however, for it eventually caused demand to evaporate when other, cheaper sources were found. Sugar from the wealthy French colony of Saint-Domingue (Haiti) and cane grown by the Dutch in Java rivalled the Barbadian product in quality, as the soil of Barbados was becoming

The plantocracy in the Caribbean. (Lennox Honychurch, *The Caribbean People*, vol. 2 [London: Thomas Nelson and Sons, 1980].)

exhausted, and its sugar of less worth. Meanwhile, in Europe in the 1740s a Prussian chemist developed a process to derive sugar from beets. The ascendancy of the West Indies was over, though Jamaica and Barbados retained their lustre for many years.

The Seven Years' War, which broke out in 1756, was a continuation of the traditional rivalry between Europe's great powers. It was, however, also a power struggle to decide who would dominate the world, and it was fought in Europe, India, North America – and the Caribbean. There was no fighting in the region for the first three years, but then a British force attacked Martinique. Resistance was too strong, however, and

A planter's ball in Jamaica. The dance was sometimes called the Creolean hop. (From the collection of the Barbados Museum and Historical Society.)

disease had affected the British ranks; the attempt failed. The same force had better luck in Guadeloupe, which they succeeded in capturing. The British refrained from looting and made no attempt to interfere with the islanders' Catholicism. The same terms were applied when Martinique fell, in 1761, to Admiral George Rodney. His force briskly seized Havana also, and with it much of the Spanish navy.

The capture of Martinique deprived France of its principal base in the West Indies. There was thus no further fighting in the Caribbean during the two years that remained before peace was restored. The Treaty of Paris in 1763 ended France's prospects of world power: it lost Canada and virtually all its possessions in India. Within the Caribbean, France at least regained Guadeloupe and Martinique, while Havana was returned to Spain. The treaty gave to Britain Dominica, Grenada, the Grenadines, St Lucia, St Vincent and Tobago, as well as Florida, which was ceded to Britain by Spain in exchange for Cuba.

Revolutions and Republics

For half a generation there was relative calm but, as so often in the past, the outcome of one conflict guaranteed the inevitability of the next, because the losers were left with grievances and a desire for revenge. Neither France nor Spain was now strong enough to challenge British naval power in the West Indies; it was only when an internal British quarrel – the American War of Independence, which began in 1776 – developed into a major war that Britain's traditional enemies saw an opportunity that could be exploited. The American rebels received a great deal of sympathy, not only from British planters and merchants in the islands but also from the governments of Britain's rivals. France and Holland both made commercial treaties with the American Congress, and the French provided military assistance, even before joining the war as their ally in 1778. Both powers allowed American privateers to use their islands for concealment and re-supply.

France sent a fleet sufficiently large to give it naval superiority in the region. It captured Dominica, which, along with Guadeloupe and Martinique, gave Britain's enemy a strategic base in the middle of the West Indian island chain from which to conduct hostilities. The French captured St Vincent, but the British retained St Lucia. Spain, joining the war as another American ally, also sent a fleet to the West Indies, though disease attacked the crews before the British could do so, and their contribution to the war was minimal.

Admiral Rodney, who twenty years earlier had captured Martinique, was once more in Caribbean waters. He sailed to the Dutch island of St Eustatius, whose inhabitants did not know that the Netherlands had just declared war on Britain. Since the American rebellion had begun, that island had been a major source of supplies for the rebels, and numerous British ships had been attracted to trade illicitly with the United States. Rodney's force arrived without warning on the morning of 3 February 1781 and annexed the island, impounding all shipping and goods. The wealth obtained from this operation was immense.

Rodney unwisely spent almost four months on the island instead of pursuing the French fleet, which was thus able to elude him. The French captured Tobago, and Rodney, who was less than a day's sail away, did not come to the island's rescue. His failure was to prove costly. Not only did his opponent, Admiral de Grasse, retake St Eustatius and St Martin, he also sailed north to the coast of Virginia, where he was in time to blockade the British army in Yorktown, forcing Lord Cornwallis to surrender to General Washington.

In April 1782, however, Rodney redeemed his reputation. Pursuing the French fleet, he found de Grasse's ships escorting a large convoy of infantry and artillery on their way to capture Jamaica. This fat prize was caught in the channel between Dominica and Guadeloupe and brought to battle. The fleets deployed in two lines. Rodney's force turned and sailed into the French line, cutting it in two places and isolating the middle, which was then pounded with broadsides from both directions until de Grasse surrendered. This "Battle of the Saints" (named after a nearby group of small islands) was not, however, a decisive victory. Most of the French ships survived and fled, avoiding capture because the British commander and his subordinates did not react quickly enough to catch them. Nevertheless, the French artillery was seized, the attack on Jamaica was aborted and – because no further attempt was mounted – the British islands were saved from French aggression. Although Rodney was condemned by the British Admiralty for his lack of initiative, he became a hero in the West Indies; the Jamaicans, having more reason than others to be grateful, took up a public subscription to build a monument to him in Kingston.

The war had also affected Nicaragua. A scheme was conceived to force a passage through the isthmus to the Pacific. This involved an expedition up the San Juan River with English soldiers carried in boats crewed by sailors and guided by Miskito Indians. They were to secure control of Lake Nicaragua by capturing a Spanish-held fort there and then move on to the Pacific coast. This misguided venture proved expensive. Progress upriver through the steaming jungle was extremely slow, and disease quickly reduced the expedition's numbers. Three-quarters of the way to their objective,

Statue of Admiral Horatio Nelson, Barbados. This bronze statue, erected in Upper Broad Street, Bridgetown, on 22 March 1813, was paid for by subscription by people from all walks of life. It was not until the 1840s that the British began to erect their own monument to Nelson in London's Trafalgar Square.

the fort was taken and briefly held, but there were not sufficient fit men to continue, and the twin threats of fever and a Spanish counter-attack persuaded the English to abandon their gains. The chief significance of the expedition was the young Royal Navy officer who led it until, on the way upriver, he was forced back by sickness: Captain Horatio Nelson.

The American War of Independence ended in 1783. As with the Seven Years' War, the peace treaty was signed in France. Now Britain gave back St Lucia and Tobago, and France gave up Dominica, Grenada, the Grenadines, Montserrat, Nevis, St Kitts and St Vincent. The safety of British loggers was also guaranteed. Having recovered from the Nicaraguan sortie, Nelson served on the Leeward Islands station. Based in Antigua, in the aftermath of the war his principal duty was to enforce compliance with the Navigation Acts. A conscientious officer, he pursued this with conspicuous zeal, and as a result became deeply unpopular with the local merchants and planters. He did, however, marry a local widow, Frances (Fanny) Nisbet, in a ceremony on the island of Nevis. The bride was given away by a friend and fellow Royal Navy captain, the Duke of Clarence, later to become King William IV.

CHAPTER 5
Britain's Fight for Supremacy over France

Britain assembles a large expeditionary force to recapture French territories in the West Indies.

Within a few years of the American Revolution there was another upheaval, farther away from the West Indies but with equally profound effects. In 1789 the French monarchy was overthrown and France became a republic. Though it rapidly developed into a police state and gained international odium by executing the former king, Louis XVI, its ideology proved an inspiration to oppressed peoples all over the world. The French colonies in the West Indies were thrown into turmoil. Despite the Revolution's emphasis on the rights of man, France did not emancipate slaves in its colonies until 1794. This was prompted by the successful slave revolt in Saint-Domingue (Haiti) in 1791 and realization that the French colonies in the Caribbean would otherwise fall to the British. This emancipation provoked widespread discontent and rebellion among slaves elsewhere. In Martinique mulattoes were granted legal equality with whites, but then were deprived of it. The consequence was a war that became racial when the black slaves joined in. Some Dutch colonies had invited British troops into their territory to forestall invasion by the French, and in Saint-Domingue the French royalists were so fearful of revolutionary forces that they too asked the British to occupy their half of Hispaniola. This was done, and the territory was held for three years, in spite of a virulent fever epidemic.

The French Republic had declared war on the United Kingdom in 1793. Two years later, Holland was conquered by France, and Dutch possessions such as Ceylon, the Cape of Good Hope and Java fell into British hands. No sooner had slaves in the French territories been freed than they were armed by the revolutionary authorities; like the whites, they were conscripted into the army – just as in metropolitan France – to defend the new regime. This force recaptured Guadeloupe and St Lucia from the British in 1795, and French agitation succeeded in igniting rebellions in St Vincent, Grenada and Dominica. When the Maroons of Jamaica also revolted, the whole region began to seem alarmingly unstable. The unrest had led to a sharp decrease in crop production in the affected islands, and this was depriving the war effort of essential funds. If Barbados and, above all, Jamaica were to descend into anarchy, the economy of the United Kingdom and its ability to wage war would be severely affected.

British troops in the Caribbean were now fighting their traditional enemy. They were helped to a limited extent by French royalists, whose contribution in no way obviated the need for a very large force to be despatched to the West Indies. Britain's sources of wealth had to be secured and France deprived of its own. No matter what perils Britain faced in Europe, Prime Minister William Pitt's Cabinet determined that this was the most immediate and pressing task. To this end the largest expeditionary force that Britain had sent overseas was assembled: thirty-three thousand troops were sent across the Atlantic to recapture French territory, protect British colonies and trade and inflict whatever economic damage on the enemy that opportunities presented. An expedition this immense could not be deployed in a single journey, so troops arrived in the West Indies in batches throughout the spring of 1796. Some, indeed, did not reach the Western Hemisphere at all. Driven back by storms and then kept waiting in England, they were eventually diverted to India, where they fought against the pro-French native ruler Tipu Sultan. Among them was Colonel Arthur Wellesley and his Thirty-third

Regiment; saved thus from a likely death in the fever-ridden Caribbean, he went on to achieve great fame in India and the Peninsular and Waterloo campaigns. He later became the Duke of Wellington.

Recognition of the Black Soldier

The Caribbean force was commanded by General Sir Ralph Abercromby. His men did well, and the blacks his force employed as labourers and auxiliaries impressed him greatly with their fortitude, loyalty and physical robustness. Sir Ralph clearly recognized the value of this manpower resource and became the leading advocate for raising black regiments and incorporating them into the British Army. His force captured Dutch Guiana in April, St Lucia a month later and Trinidad at the beginning of the following year. Over the next few years they went on to seize Curaçao, St Martin and the Danish West Indies. They also put down revolts in St Vincent and Grenada. The Maroon rebellion in Jamaica had already collapsed, in part because of the use of slave-catching dogs imported from the Spanish islands.

Like the Seven Years' War, this conflict had developed into what was effectively a world war. Though it was naturally in Europe that the most decisive events took place, the Caribbean was a vital theatre of operations. Because their colonies in the area were the greatest source of wealth for both sides (they handled a fifth of Britain's overseas trade and more than a quarter of France's), each side sought to deprive the other of its resources. The terrain was more difficult than anything encountered in Europe, for armies had to negotiate mountains and dense, sweltering jungle, with malarial swamps as additional hazards.

This was not a type of warfare that suited the traditional drill and training of British soldiers. The landscape of jungle and mountain prevented armies from deploying in ordered ranks and fighting major battles as they would have done in Europe. Instead there were continuous skirmishes, minor engagements and attacks on forts. Not all troops fell foul of conditions; one

Maroons in negotiation with a British officer. (James Carnegie and Patricia Patterson, *The People Who Came*, vol. 2 [Edinburgh: Pearson Educational, 1989].)

force, commanded by Sir Charles Grey, contained men who had seen this type of combat in the American Revolution, and they proved highly effective. Nevertheless, fever was an enemy more to be feared than the French. Campaigning was not possible during the hottest months, but at all times the men were prone to illness, whether they were in the field or languishing in barracks. A succession of abnormally humid summers during the 1790s multiplied the mosquito population, and thus the chances of perishing from disease, though the mosquito's role in infecting human beings was not yet understood.

Deadly Diseases: The Real Enemy

During much of its recorded history the West Indies were a perfect environment for deadly and crippling diseases. Constantly warm sea-level temperatures and abundant water were the chief factors contributing to the lethality of the area. From the seventeenth to the eighteenth centuries this lethality increased dramatically, and when newcomers entered the region they encountered a host of mysterious and deadly diseases; yellow fever, malaria, dengue and dysentery were the leading killers. Moreover, the best medical minds of the era were ignorant of the causes of these fevers, making cures more difficult. Some useful vital facts gradually became known: malaria miasmas were found near swamps; yellow fever was an urban disease; non-immune Europeans were the most vulnerable; on the hills and mountain ridges, where the air was cool, Europeans thrived; and, above all, that the anopheles mosquito was the principal culprit in transmitting malaria and yellow fever to human beings.

"New rum" was the other deadly menace to Europeans. Often the rum they drank was improperly distilled and came from machinery with a high lead content. This toxic combination proved fatal to many, and things were made worse by the belief that drinking rum would prevent yellow fever.

In the ten-year period between 1793 and 1803, some 1,500 officers and 43,500 other ranks of the British Army died from fevers while in the Caribbean. The worst year proved to be 1796, when 41 per cent of soldiers died within a year of arrival.[1] The vast area of the Caribbean and the number of territories that needed to be captured, defended or garrisoned meant that, in the twenty-two years between the outbreak of war and the defeat of Napoleon in 1815, 95,000 soldiers fought for Britain in the region. Of these, 89,000 were white and 45,000 of them – almost exactly half – died. More than nine out of every ten of these were victims of disease rather than enemy action. One observer, Sir John Hope, recalled that, for men loaded with equipment and dressed in the same uniforms they wore at home, "a man is apt to feel himself languid and enfeebled, and under the pressure of disease every ache, every pain is doubled by that lassitude which is the universal attachment of loss of health here".

Losses on this scale were unsustainable, and morale among British troops posted to the West Indies was abysmal. Desertion was so commonplace and mutiny such a danger in regiments waiting to embark, that it was sometimes necessary to tell the men they were going somewhere else in order to get them aboard ship. In 1795 Dr Pinckard wrote: "a degree of horror [seemed] to have overspread the nation, from the late disastrous effects of the seasoning fever or what the multitude denominate the West India Plague; insomuch that a sense of terror attaches to it the very name of the West Indies". As persons looked on they were overheard to exclaim, "Ah poor fellow! You are going to your last home! What a pity that such brave men shall go to that West India grave – to that hateful climate to be killed by the plague! Poor fellow, Goodby, farewell: We shall never see you again . . . ."[2]

Black Soldiers

Slaves were again proving loyal and courageous, and it was at this time that black regiments began to be formed in an attempt to reduce the losses among white troops. A "Carolina Corps" had previously been created of Loyalist African Americans, and this type of locally raised unit was seen as better suited to the climate, the terrain and the semi-guerrilla nature of the fighting. The prospect of armed and trained black soldiers met with predictable opposition among the planters, but these units represented such a saving in British lives that the secretary of state for war, Henry Dundas, gained the king's approval for eventual establishment of twelve such regiments. "Recruits" were obtained by buying the fittest available Negroes at £70 a head, but many slave owners showed their displeasure by refusing to release those whom the army wanted. As a result it became easier to fill the ranks with men bought in West Africa or taken off foreign slave ships that the Royal Navy had arrested. While many of the slaves thus obtained ended up serving in units of the West India Regiment (WIR), a large number were employed by British regiments garrisoning the islands. Some, specially honoured by the title "the King's Negroes", became skilled artisans and craftsmen, others served as labourers and fatigue-men in the various military camps and forts, and still others served as officers' servants (army regulations entitled majors to have three servants, captains two and humble ensigns one each).

In 1795 a regiment called the Corps of Loyal Black Rangers was raised in Grenada, and Martinique had a similar body of troops. During that year the creation of eight black regiments was authorized. These men were not nearly as prone to disease as the Europeans, and their units were therefore not constantly being whittled away by fever. They were also less liable to desert and drunkenness was far less common. They were paid at the same rate as European troops, given the same food and housed in the same type of barracks; not having to be transported from England, they were economical. However, though the men had a certain status as soldiers, they were still legally classified as slaves and were seen as such when outside their barracks. One regiment, raised in St Lucia in 1797, saw service in Africa, though most, naturally, were deployed in the West Indies. They could not, however, be posted everywhere: the planter-controlled governments of both Jamaica and Barbados refused to allow black troops to be stationed on their territory.

These black soldiers, who at the beginning of the new century numbered ten thousand in twelve regiments, won laurels. After the capture of the Dutch/French island of St Martin, a British officer, Lieutenant-General Thomas Trigge, described one of the units in these terms:

I have particular satisfaction in being enabled to add that the 8th West India Regiment, formed within the last three years, and composed almost entirely of new Negroes, who had never before seen an enemy, engaged with a degree of gallantry, and behaved in a manner, that would honour any troops.[3]

By the end of 1801 the Royal Navy was in command of the seas and the oceans, was keeping the ports and coastal waters of France under close blockade, and dominated the West Indies. But Napoleon had gained his objectives in Europe and peace was agreed. In the resulting Treaty of Amiens, Britain gave back most of the French territories it had captured during the hostilities. The interlude of peace was brief, for war resumed the following year and the capturing of enemy territory began again.

Napoleon wanted to restore French power – and slavery – in the West Indies. He also realized that, to defeat Britain, he had to invade England. To do this he had to draw the Royal Navy far from European waters so that his army could cross the English Channel unopposed. If his fleets could elude the blockade and cross the Atlantic, the British would pursue them. Two of his three fleets did get away, though not concentrated as Bonaparte had ordered, and they caused a great deal of anxiety in the Caribbean, where some islands paid stiff ransoms to avoid pillage. When the second fleet, commanded by Admiral Villeneuve, set out to join the first in the West Indies, it was closely followed by the British Mediterranean fleet, led by Lord Nelson. To avoid a battle so far from Europe, Villeneuve abandoned plans to attack Barbados and other British islands and headed back across the Atlantic, but he found the approaches to the Channel barred by other Royal Navy ships. He took refuge in Spanish waters and Nelson returned briefly to England. Some months later, on 21 October 1805, Nelson brought to battle the combined (and stronger) Franco-Spanish fleet off Cape Trafalgar, near Cadiz, and destroyed it.

After Trafalgar there would be no major naval battle in the West Indies, because Nelson's relentless pursuit of Villeneuve had removed the major threat to Britain's sources of wealth there. Indeed, the West Indies were now beyond France's reach. Its colonies, and those of its Spanish, Dutch and Danish allies, were stranded, and many fell again into British hands. In this second phase of the war against Emperor Napoleon's France there was no need to recreate the massive expeditionary force of the 1790s. By this time the West India regiments were sufficiently established to form a third of the British Army's garrisons in the region. Moreover, conditions for white soldiers had improved markedly thanks to medical research and more skilled treatment; by then much more was being done to prepare units to cope with the problems of climate and disease in the Caribbean. Incentives in the form of fast promotion and more prize money also did something to raise morale, and the soldier of the early nineteenth century had a better prospect of survival than his counterpart of a generation earlier. In 1796 the casualty rate had been 41 per cent; by 1810 it had fallen to less than 14 per cent.

When the war in Europe ended in 1814, Britain gave back most of the territories it had gained (with the exception of St Lucia and Tobago). It had undisputed control of the Caribbean trade, though for economic reasons this would soon lose much of its importance. A significant consequence of the Napoleonic Wars, and of the long era of peace that Europe enjoyed after 1815, was the colonial peoples' struggles against Spanish rule on the South American mainland from 1810 to 1830. In these successful wars for independence, some British soldiers and sailors – discharged from the forces after Napoleon's defeat at Waterloo – volunteered to play a part. In Central America the picture was different. In 1847 the "War of the Castes" between the Mayan Indians and their Spanish overlords broke out in the Yucatán Peninsula; it was to last more than two decades. This had a considerable impact on the administrative and military resources of British Honduras (now Belize), which was also being attacked by a series of Mayan raids from across the border. The fighting ended only in 1872, when the First WIR successfully fought off the Icaiche people.

CHAPTER 6
Self-Defence: The Militia

The defence and policing of the Caribbean territories was an impractical proposition without the support of locally raised white and black militias.

The militia – an emergency-service military force made up of trained local citizens – was a concept that was deeply embedded in the culture of European nations, where it was a natural successor to the feudal military obligations of the medieval peasantry. The government in London lost no time in extending it to the white population of the West Indian islands claimed by Britain, and very quickly after their settlement or capture militia units were in place. The Caribbean's volatile situation made this absolutely imperative. Without large numbers of regular soldiers in the region, the burden of defence fell largely on the white planters and farmers. The home government was both unwilling and unable to provide permanent garrisons, and nothing therefore stood between the English islanders and their country's enemies but the military skills they could learn and practise.

Dangers in the islands that did not exist at home could give a vital urgency to the drilling and training of these local units. International tensions – whether or not war had been formally declared – meant that the ships and soldiers of rival powers might descend at any time to plunder towns or plantations, burn crops, capture slaves or hold communities to ransom. Apart from these official enemies, who were acting at least nominally on behalf of distant governments, pirates might cause similar mayhem on their own account. And there were other predators; Antigua and Montserrat, for instance, were subject to raids by Caribs during the 1670s. An additional element caused greater alarm even than these: the prospect of slave rebellion was a constant factor in military and political life from the seventeenth to the nineteenth century. The existence of well-armed auxiliary units was an extremely effective deterrent.

Militias required the service of all able-bodied white men aged between sixteen and sixty (a fairly advanced age at that time, and an indication of the pressing need for men). These included indentured servants, who were usually so badly treated by their masters that they could not be expected to defend them with any enthusiasm. When Spanish forces sought to drive English settlers from St Kitts and Nevis in 1629, the refusal of these poorer whites to fight meant that resistance collapsed and their leaders had to negotiate. A contemporary observer recorded that the militia deserted at the first opportunity, and that "ye most of them, being indentured, cried out 'Liberty, joyfull liberty'" – clearly regarding their country's enemies as less of a threat than their own superiors.

Initially the militias included a large number of smallholders – "five and ten acre men" – who possessed the same stolid courage as their counterparts among the yeoman-farmers of England. As the economy became increasingly monopolized by large-scale plantations, the smaller landowners were gradually squeezed out of their livelihoods, and the militia units came to be dominated by men of lower military calibre from among the poor whites. Island militias were organized into regiments and companies, commanded by prominent local figures who held commissions from the governor, but while the officer class enjoyed the prestige of command, their troops displayed widespread reluctance. Militias underwent training at least once a month and often practised drill every week, but in spite of the threats to their security, service was often unpopular. The constant imposition of martial law and calling up of the troops, time spent watching from headlands for approaching enemy ships or guarding buildings and communities in times of slave unrest – all could mean significant loss of income. One observer commented: "The frequent occasion of martial law, by which the ordinary people are kept on duty instead of being at work to earn their bread . . . makes them retire to the Northern Colonies for greater ease and quiet."[1]

Militia members were expected to furnish their own weapons and ammunition, and, when at a later stage uniforms were introduced, these too had to be paid for by the men themselves. Though initially all members of these organizations were white, the understandable reluctance of men to serve in them, as well as a lack of manpower (the white population declined significantly during the eighteenth century), led them gradually and increasingly to include free coloureds and free blacks, whose legal standing as freemen obliged them to serve in any case. This section of society could well have taken to militia service with a greater sense of commitment, for it was not only a badge of status but also a necessity. Free blacks had as much to fear from a slave uprising as any white person, and they ran a high risk of kidnap if pirates or foreign troops made a raid in search of blacks to sell as slaves. In fact, however, they were equally reluctant to serve. Many were involved in trade and manufacture, and they resented as much as anyone else the interruption of their work. Their opportunity for greater status did not in any case extend to eligibility for officer rank; they were always commanded by whites. Slaves too were involved in the militia, after a fashion; they often carried their masters' weapons on exercises and even in actual fighting. As was the case with regular soldiers, they were also called upon to build defences and undertake other menial work because of their greater aptitude for heavy work in the climate.

Driven by ideology and motivation, however, a militia could compare well with professional soldiers. The issues that divided England and led to the civil wars of the 1640s naturally had echoes in the West Indies. In Barbados the militia was efficiently reorganized by an officer, Captain Philip Bell, to fight for the king. Within its ranks were many former royalist soldiers who had been transported to the island by Parliament. These were the defenders of Barbados who put up such a strong resistance to the parliamentary force sent to subdue the island. In the years following

the Restoration the militias remained important, for conflict with
the Dutch brought further threats to peace, perpetuating the need
for their members to neglect fields and businesses in order to keep
watch or to wait in readiness for alarms. Many islands maintained
substantial forces in relation to their population: Montserrat mustered eight hundred men, Nevis a thousand and Antigua eleven
hundred. In the 1660s Barbados reached a strength of eleven thousand – though this was later almost halved – of whom a thousand
were cavalry, and the governor even boasted a seventy-man personal escort, or "life guard".

In Jamaica Charles II agreed to offer a thirty-acre land grant to
all new settlers, provided they were willing to undertake military
service in instances of "insurrection, mutiny or forraine invasion".[2]
This need for men was exacerbated by trouble with the Maroons,
whose mountainous stronghold was proving too difficult for
amateur soldiers to breach. Militia acts, passed by the assembly
in Kingston but not energetically enforced, enabled many men to
avoid service, and the problem of the Maroons simply worsened
until the middle of the following century, when regular troops
made a determined – but not entirely successful – attempt to deal
with it. But while the Jamaica militia proved ineffectual against
the rugged terrain and guerrilla tactics of the Maroons, they demonstrated noticeable valour when confronted with "forraine invasion" and the need to protect their homes. In 1694 a force of
French regular troops landed on the island. With no prospect of
naval or military assistance, the militia put up a desperate defence
that wore down the French attack. Their progress stalled and the
initiative lost, the invaders could see no prospect of success, and
withdrew. Again it had been proved that with sufficient incentive
– and perhaps the bonus of a few good officers – a militia could
prove a match for regulars.

Of those who did serve in the militia ranks, many seemed highly
dubious. William III had a number of Monmouth rebels, who had
been transported to the West Indies after the 1685 rebellion failed,
released from ten-year sentences as indentured labourers in order
to assist with the islands' defence. Militia formations were also, as
the historian Sir Alan Burns noted, "composed mainly of servants

The band of the Barbados Defence Force in Zouave uniform at the Edinburgh Tattoo.

without a stake in the country, many of them being Irish Catholics who were suspected of being disloyal and ready to join in any revolt or with any invader against the Government".[3]

While the lower ranks might be considered riff-raff, the officers were normally wealthy planters and other men of local commercial importance, and they had a sense of their own fitness to command that reflected their economic power. Their units were often absurdly top-heavy with officers; in one instance an Antiguan "regiment" fielded only a hundred men, but it had four lieutenants, four captains, two majors, two lieutenant-colonels and a colonel. In another case a company consisted of only four members: a colonel, a lieutenant, an ensign and a private. For the officer class, exemptions from service were often easy to obtain, and for those in positions of authority who neglected their duty, punishments were usually half-hearted. The result was an endemic and widespread lack of effectiveness.

It was not only the militias but the regular army as well that suffered from a shortage of manpower throughout this era. As Roger Buckley points out in his seminal work, *Slaves in Red Coats*,

Several crosscurrents adversely affected white recruitment during the eighteenth century. Economic restrictions on military spending, the absence of conscription, and the unpopularity of employing regulars to aid the civil power at home (as well as the unpopularity of lifetime service) prevented the maintenance of a British standing army large enough to satisfy expanding demands.

If soldiers were unwilling to serve in the West Indies and if the British public was unenthusiastic about having a sizeable regular army, the local populations of Caribbean islands also had reservations, for they were expected to bear much of the expense of maintaining a garrison. The solution had two aspects: the recruitment of black regular troops and the employment of more blacks in the militia. Buckley continues:

A dwindling white population, coupled with failure to maintain an acceptable black–white demographic ratio, made the induction of free blacks and coloureds into the colonial militia a practical necessity; by the middle of the eighteenth century the practice had been adopted almost everywhere in the Caribbean. The European wars of the late eighteenth century and the concomitant colonial struggles accelerated employment of blacks in both colonial and imperial military services.[4]

Black soldiers thus became an increasingly common sight in the islands. Those in command made it a deliberate policy to develop feelings of both corporate and individual pride in these men. Their military training put them a cut above the slave "pioneers" used in some islands (in Jamaica two were assigned to every company of troops) for building fortifications and other manual military tasks, and gave them a status almost unimaginable to slaves outside the army. By encouraging a sense of superiority over other blacks, it was expected that they would not make common cause with them, and that in slave uprisings this would ensure their loyalty to the government.

The loyalty of both black and white militia members – as well as their courage and skill – was put to the test on several occasions during the eighteenth century. While their counterparts in Britain fired off practice volleys on commons and village greens,

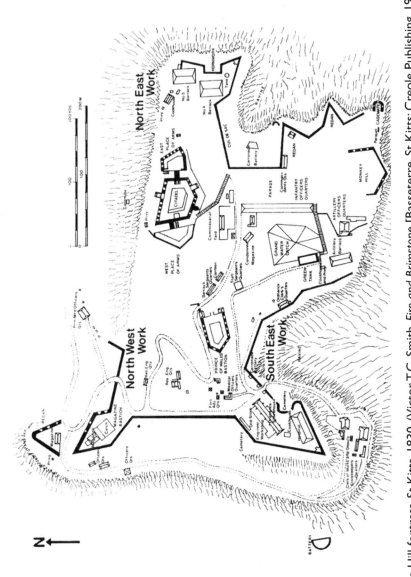

Brimstone Hill fortress, St Kitts, 1830. (Victor T.C. Smith, *Fire and Brimstone* [Basseterre, St Kitts: Creole Publishing, 1992].)

the amateur soldiers of the West Indies could expect to hear shots fired in earnest. The Seven Years' War, like all conflicts between the European maritime powers, quickly made an impact in the Caribbean. The American Revolution, which swiftly widened into a full-scale war against Britain's traditional rivals, once again brought hostile fleets and armies over the horizon to strangle commerce, interrupt planting and destroy property. While the citizenry of an island might sue for peace, the soldiery – regulars and militia – would make an attempt at resistance. This happened in July 1779, when a French fleet commanded by Admiral d'Estaing attacked Grenada. A force of 400 militia and 125 regulars barricaded themselves inside forts, where they held out for four days before having to ask for terms. Two years later French troops landed in St Kitts, where the town of Basseterre was given up to the invaders and the garrison, together with the militia, retreated inside the fortress at Brimstone Hill. Unfortunately the artillery pieces intended for the island's defence were still at the harbour, where the French found them and used them to besiege and capture the fortress.

Also in 1781, French troops landed in Tobago to meet spirited and effective resistance from a motley force of more than four hundred locals and a group of blacks "who behaved with undaunted courage in some desperate service".[5] The defenders withdrew to a ridge, where they dug in. Here they could have defied the enemy for some time, had two factors not defeated them. First, the relief they expected from Admiral Rodney's ships did not materialize. Second, the French proceeded to burn plantations within sight of their owners on the ridge. Militiamen began to slip away from the defences to salvage their property, and the resistance was fatally weakened.

By the 1790s there was war once again, but this time the situation was more sinister. The events in France in 1789 had added to the customary international plundering an element of social anarchy. Slaves throughout the region saw an opportunity to free themselves and assume equality according to revolutionary principles, which France had promised to spread throughout the world. Britain needed all its available troops at home to protect its own shores, so the Caribbean could rely even less than previously on assistance from the mother country. Those regulars who did reach the area fell foul of the climate as swiftly as usual (General Charles Grey, commander of a force that arrived in the summer of 1794, reported to Whitehall that 1,359 of his men had become unfit for service over a four-week period). The organizing, arming and training of island militias therefore became noticeably less lackadaisical. New regulations tightened discipline and smartened up appearances, prescribing uniforms, facings, buttons and badges that brought a greater *esprit de corps* to these amateur units. Regiments of black regulars were also raised, and endowed with a similar ethos.

By the turn of the nineteenth century the steady addition of black soldiers to their ranks had given the islands some sizeable militia units. Grenada boasted five regiments of infantry, two artillery companies and a troop of light dragoons. Trinidad had infantry and cavalry regiments. Jamaica mustered the Caribbean's largest militia, with fourteen regiments of infantry (by 1803 there would be eighteen) and three of cavalry, a total of eleven thousand men, of whom three thousand were free blacks. Even the woodcutters of British Honduras had a loosely organized militia. Its members may have lacked the smart uniforms of their comrades in other territories, but they made up for this with shooting skill. Very unusually their unit contained armed slaves, who were described as "superb marksmen". They made a major and decisive contribution to the defeat of Spanish invaders at the battle of St George's Caye in 1798.

In territories that the British annexed or conquered, desperation led them to incorporate the local militias of other powers, as happened in Guadeloupe, Martinique, St Lucia and St Domingo. In all cases the locals showed either marked reluctance or open hostility to the notion of serving the new power, and both threats and inducements were largely ignored.

The defeat of the French and Spanish fleets at Trafalgar in October 1805 was an event of vast significance for the Caribbean. It gave Britain undisputed control of the region and meant that its rivals were, in military terms, cut off from their possessions in the Western Hemisphere. The war thus effectively ended in the

West Indies a decade earlier than it did in Europe. But, almost a decade later, when Britain was in conflict with the United States, the militias were once again placed on a war footing, their troops drilling twice a week. The islands, however, played no direct role in these hostilities, and – with the exception of "police duties", most significantly during slave uprisings – were not deployed in any serious situation again. Ironically the Napoleonic conflict had brought the West Indian militia units to the highest level of training, smartness and efficiency that they had yet attained – at the very moment that the region was losing its economic and strategic importance.

CHAPTER 7
The Emancipation Era

New consciousness among the slaves of independence and freedom. A heroine emerges from Jamaica.

By the time Napoleon was defeated in 1815, important changes had already taken place in the Caribbean. Slavery – the system that underpinned the entire local economy – was becoming increasingly unsustainable. The revolutions in America and France had profoundly altered the outlook of many people across the world. The uprisings against Spanish rule throughout South and Central America were sparked by this new awareness of the concept of independence and the notion that Man – any man – was entitled to dignity and basic rights. The most extreme instances were the slave revolts throughout the region and the overthrow of French authority in Saint-Domingue (Haiti), which became an independent republic on 1 January 1804. Though the slave leader, Toussaint L'Ouverture, had a short career that ended in imprisonment and death in France, his brief period of ascendancy showed the way for others. He was followed by a self-styled emperor, Henri Christophe, who established appropriate trappings of pomp and power – a court, an aristocracy and a system of protocol – that must have seemed to Europeans (in the words of a contemporary popular song) a "world turned upside down". Blacks in the West Indies would never again see themselves in the same light.

In fact, the whole climate of opinion about slavery was changing. Some European countries began by abolishing trading in slaves;

Denmark did so in 1803, Britain in 1807, the United States in 1808 and France in 1817. Britain made slavery illegal within its empire in 1833, and had already sent the Royal Navy to West Africa to arrest foreign vessels bringing human cargo across the Atlantic. France abolished slavery after the revolution of 1848. Other nations chose a suitable moment according to their economic circumstances and the dictates of public opinion at home: the Dutch in 1818, Sweden in 1846 and the Spanish islands of Puerto Rico and Cuba in 1870 and 1880 respectively. In the United States slavery was ended by the Union victory in the American Civil War (1861–65). In Brazil it was abolished in 1888.

A slave "coffle". (James Carnegie and Patricia Patterson, *The People Who Came*, vol. 2 [Edinburgh: Pearson Educational, 1989].)

Increasingly regarded by international opinion as unacceptable, slavery was also uneconomical. The fact that slaves were more expensive to feed, house and look after than free workers was an important factor in the willingness of planters to acquiesce in their emancipation. The estate owners were, in any case, no longer the nabobs they had been in the previous century. They soon turned to employing – under slave conditions – indentured labourers. But competition from other regions – the Dutch had

A slave auction. (Lennox Honychurch, *The Caribbean People*, vol. 2 [London: Thomas Nelson and Sons, 1980].)

developed cultivation of cane sugar in Java, and sugar beets were now widely grown in Europe – had effectively ended the reign of the all-powerful wealthy plantocracy that had dominated some islands for almost two hundred years. In many cases the price paid for sugar had become less than the cost of producing it. Now the estates were no longer cost-effective to run, and many were up for sale.

Emancipation was, as we have seen, a process that spread only gradually through the region. This caused the black populations of British possessions to become impatient. They expected their freedom to be granted instantly and imagined that every new governor arriving from Britain carried the necessary proclamation in his pocket. Instead their condition improved only by stages. Use of the whip was abolished and limits were put on the work that women, children and the elderly could be made to do. Blacks who lived in the territories of nations where slavery was still legal could – and often did – escape and make their way to "free" islands, where they too automatically became free. Knowing full well that their future status was being debated by the governments of the home countries, their impatience led to a number of disturbances. In Barbados, Jamaica and some other islands, the militia or the WIR had to be called out on several occasions to put down disorder.

Within a few years of emancipation, Queen Victoria came to the throne. Her reign (1837–1901) was to mark the zenith of British power and prestige and was largely free of international conflicts. Though not free of regional unrest and social tensions in the Caribbean, this was the first such peace the region had known since the arrival of Columbus. With cane sugar no longer the vital and lucrative commodity it had been, the islands ceased to be the equivalent of modern-day oilfields. The region had lost its former strategic value, and Nelson's victory at Trafalgar had swept from the world's oceans all rivals to British maritime supremacy. In fact, the West Indies were seen as having little value to anyone. The decline of sugar meant that many estates were sold and broken up, and the land was often bought by coloureds and cultivated in smaller units. This not only made the colonies' agriculture more diverse but spread wealth more widely among the population, so that small landowners became more prosperous and influential.

Nevertheless, the cultivation of sugar continued and indeed prospered as some planters, notably in the southern Caribbean, resorted to improved agricultural and manufacturing technologies. Similar advances were made in Trinidad and British Guiana, but there the planters suffered from a labour shortage. Their remedies led to vital social consequences. Within a year the first Portuguese labourers arrived from Madeira, and coolies from India were imported into the West Indies (ever since, they have been known as East Indians). By 1917, 239,000 Indian immigrants had arrived in British Guiana, 134,000 in Trinidad and many others in Jamaica and its sister islands. These immigrants were given the option of repatriation after completing their five years of indenture, but most elected to remain. After 1850, Chinese workers were also brought in, but they, like the Portuguese, soon left the cane fields for more lucrative employment.

As their links with their mother countries weakened, the newcomers increasingly regarded themselves as West Indians, and education enabled them to rise to high positions in their new homes. In this way the nineteenth century saw West Indian society became dangerously segregated into three tiers, distinguished by race as well as by wealth and occupation: the white plutocracy, the coloured middle class and the black working class. Moreover, in British Guiana and in Trinidad this working class became ominously subdivided into Negro and East Indian elements, and when disturbances occurred they would erupt violently along racial fissures. Thus the immigration policies of the post-abolition period shaped some of the present-day features of Caribbean life.

A West Indian Heroine: Mary Seacole

In the midst of this century, which was for the Caribbean an incongruous mix of international peace and some local turbulence, the region produced a heroine whose name is still an inspiration both in her native Jamaica and in Britain. Mary Jane Grant was born in 1805; it was a brief marriage (she was soon widowed) to a godson of Lord Nelson that gave her the name by which she became better known: Mary Seacole.

Mary Seacole was the daughter of a black Jamaican and a Scottish army officer. Her mother ran a hotel in Kingston that was popular with naval and military officers, but she also practised "medicine" – most commonly, herbal medicine – a common occupation among women in that era. Growing up in this atmosphere, Mary acquired both her mother's management skills – she became a successful businesswoman early in life – and her ability as a healer. Taking over the hotel in 1843, she became a well-known figure in Kingston. Seven years later her services during a cholera epidemic confirmed the respect of local people and impressed the military authorities. Always susceptible to the lure of adventure, she travelled extensively in the Western Hemisphere, visiting both North and Central America (where she was briefly a gold prospector). Mrs Seacole proved equal to the harsh living conditions of the jungle, the racial attitudes of the American South and the risk of yellow fever. In 1853 she nursed victims through a fever outbreak in Kingston, and as a result was asked to supervise the medical facilities at Up Park Camp, where the British forces in Jamaica were stationed.

Mrs Seacole made her way to England (a country she had already visited twice) in 1854 and asked permission to go to the Crimea as a nurse with the British Army, which was then fighting alongside the French against the Russians. Her offer was rejected. Undaunted, she paid her own expenses and sailed – not to Scutari in Turkey, where many of the wounded were being treated after being evacuated across the Black Sea – but to the Crimea itself. In Balaclava she set up in business with a relation, Thomas Day. She was not concerned solely with nursing the injured, but also sought to put to use her business acumen and her experience as a hotelier. The troops' rations were inadequate and they were often swindled by sellers of food and drinks. Mrs Seacole – who, after all, had to recoup the cost of her journey – set out to provide them with wholesome and clean facilities. She and Day opened the British Hotel just outside the town and it proved immediately successful. Her cooking became legendary, and both officers and men could dine there – in separate rooms, of course – at no great expense. Gambling was prohibited and so was drunkenness, but the establishment flourished nevertheless; even hardbitten war correspondents were impressed.

Mary Seacole was as unconcerned by the proximity of war as she had been by cholera and yellow fever, and she did not wait for the wounded to be brought to her from the battlefield. She frequently went to the quayside to dispense medicines (she mixed all her own) or tea to the injured who were awaiting evacuation. She also rode to the British lines to give what comfort she could to the men camped

Sculpture of Mary Seacole by George "Fowokan" Kelly, also known as George Kell. (Mia Morris, Well Placed Consultancy, http://www.black-history.co.uk)

outside Sevastopol. When the city was bombed and attacked, she was there with her supplies. She later recalled her experiences in a best-selling autobiography, which is worth quoting from at length, for it illustrates not only her personal courage and the affection with which the soldiers regarded her, but also her wry humour.

I had found out that, in the stillness of the night, many regiments were marching down to the trenches, and that the break of day would be the signal that should let them loose upon the Russians. We were all busily occupied in cutting bread and cheese and sandwiches, packing up fowls, tongues, and ham, wine and spirits, while I carefully filled the large bag, which I always carried into the field slung across my shoulder, with lint, bandages, needles, thread and medicines; and soon after day-break everything was ready packed upon two mules, in charge of my sturdiest lad, and I, leading the way on horseback, the little cavalcade left the British Hotel before the sun of the fatal 18th of June had been many hours old.

It was not long before our progress was arrested by the cavalry pickets closely stationed to stop all stragglers and spectators from reaching the scene of action. But after a slight parley, and when they found out who I was, and how I was prepared for the day's work, the men raised a shout for me, and, with their officer's sanction, allowed me to pass. Leaving the mules, I loaded myself with all the provisions I could carry, and succeeded in reaching the reserves of Sir Henry Barnard's division, which was to have stormed something, I forget what; but when they found the attack upon the Redan was a failure, very wisely abstained. Here I found plenty of officers who soon relieved me of my refreshments, and some wounded men who found the contents of my bag very useful. At length I made my way to the Worontzoff Road, where the temporary hospital had been erected, and there I found the doctors hard enough at work, and hastened to help them as best I could. I bound up the wounds and ministered to the wants of a good many, and stayed there some considerable time.

Upon the way, and even here, I was "under fire". More frequently than was agreeable, a shot would come ploughing up the ground and raising clouds of dust, or a shell whiz above us. Upon these occasions those around me would cry out "Lie down, Mother, lie down!" and with unladylike haste I had to embrace the earth, and remain there until the same voices would laughingly assure me that the danger was over, and hope that the old lady was neither hit nor frightened. Several times on that eventful day I was ordered back, but each time my bag of bandages and comforts for the wounded proved my passport. And the grateful words and smile which rewarded me for binding up a wound or giving a cooling drink was a pleasure worth risking life for at any time.[1]

When the war ended in 1856, Mrs Seacole and Day were left holding stores and equipment that were no longer needed. They suffered considerable financial loss, but when she returned to England she was feted by the public and by veterans. She was awarded a total of four medals, including the Crimean campaign medal, and several officers gave a benefit dinner in her honour. Unfortunately she received little of the money raised, and a sutler's store that she opened in Aldershot was not a success. She tried to go to India in order to work with the army there, but could not raise the necessary funds. (Queen Victoria felt that, in any case, her life was too precious to risk on a distant continent.) Nevertheless, she was not destitute; she lived, more or less in comfort, for a further quarter of a century after the war. She died in England in 1881, leaving more than £2,000, and was buried in London's Kensal Green cemetery.

Though Mary Seacole's life and achievements have been rediscovered in recent years, she is less well-known than her contemporary Florence Nightingale, who is rightly honoured as the founder of modern nursing. The British Army owes as great a debt to Mrs Seacole, however, for she pioneered the entire concept of soldiers' welfare. The British Hotel was the forerunner of various facilities that would be provided in later conflicts – and in times of peace – by the Salvation Army, the Church Army, the Young Men's Christian Association and the modern-day UK Navy, Army and Air Force Institutes. Her work in this field was also echoed unwittingly by many of her fellow West Indians almost ninety years later, when in another war they contributed money to buy mobile canteens and recreation huts for British soldiers and civilians.

CHAPTER 8
Small Wars, Peacekeeping and Heroism

The West India Regiment wins battle honours in the Caribbean; sees continuous military action in West Africa for most of the nineteenth century when unit numbers were considerably reduced.

By the end of the Napoleonic Wars, West India regiments had won battle honours in three engagements in their own region (Dominica in 1805, Martinique in 1809 and Guadeloupe in 1810) and had fought in Louisiana in an entirely separate – and unsuccessful – conflict against the United States. Several regiments had, however, been disbanded even before hostilities ended. By 1807 the twelve had been reduced to eight, and in 1816 another two were abolished. The strength of the remaining six was established at 650 men each, with a chaplain and a schoolmaster. By that time Parliament had abolished the slave trade and slaves could no longer be purchased for service in the WIR. However, it allowed the conscription of slaves being transported in other nations' ships that were captured by the Royal Navy. The troops therefore continued to come largely from West Africa (though a recruiting centre had also been established in the West Indies), and most spoke no English. Often taken en masse and enlisted effectively for life, they might well be younger than the stipulated minimum age of fifteen or less than the required height of five feet three inches.

Despite the challenge of moulding these disparate elements into an effective body of men, the officers and non-commissioned officers (NCOs) managed to instil much of the pride and cohesion that all military units hope to attain. But because they were recently formed, the WIRs were subject to the snobbery of regiments that already boasted a century or more of service, and this meant that they were never "fashionable". Nevertheless, they had a steady supply of officers who, in many cases, served with the WIR because promotion was quicker than in Britain. These officers were often with the regiments for only very short periods before transferring to other units. Because of this lack of continuity among the higher ranks, there emerged a species of capable and efficient black NCO. As is customary in the British Army, these tough and experienced men formed the backbone of their units and instilled pride as well as smartness in the recruits. For those who joined the regiment, the transition from a largely barefoot and ragged existence to a world of spit-shined tidiness and a colourful uniform was a considerable culture shock. Those who graduated into full-fledged soldiers in the WIR developed considerable swagger. They were idolized by local women and highly respected by black civilians, whom they looked upon with disdain. Those who were "King's Men", or volunteers, also looked down on their comrades who were conscripted slaves.

Like all units, the regiments had occasional bad luck with their officers. Blacks could work in the West Indian climate more easily than members of other races, and they were sometimes treated as a ready source of cheap labour. In 1802 the Eighth WIR, stationed in Dominica, mutinied because the men were ordered to carry out manual work and then were swindled by their commanding officer out of the additional pay to which this entitled them. They took over their military post, Fort Shirley, killing seven officers and taking three hostages, but they voluntarily surrendered after this initial show of anger. The rebellion was put down with a good deal of brutality, and seventy-seven members of the regiment were killed. The men understandably resented the notion that they were labourers in uniform, but this and other periodic flashes of rebellion gained the black units a reputation as troublesome and mutinous that would cause some prejudice in the next hundred years.

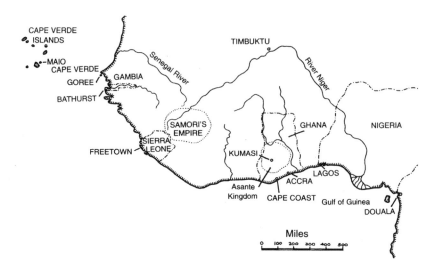

West Africa, including Ashanti (Asante). (Brian Dyde, *The Empty Sleeve: The Story of the West India Regiments of the British Army* [St John's, Antigua: Hansib Caribbean, 1997].)

In the area from which so many of the soldiers came – West Africa – a theatre of conflict was opening up that would absorb the energies of different WIR units for much of the nineteenth century. Britain occupied the coastal territory of Sierra Leone and was extending commercial and administrative control over the hinterland. This region, later to be known as the "white man's grave" because of its deadly climate, was even worse for European troops than the West Indies. As early as 1802 the British authorities, the Sierra Leone Company, requested the use of soldiers from the Caribbean, though events there meant that none could be spared. The British presence in West Africa was maintained by a combination of locally recruited former slaves and British penal units known collectively as the Royal African Corps. Local rulers, who were losing control of the river mouths, became increasingly resentful of British inter-ference and resorted to acts of non-cooperation or outright defiance.

In 1820 local rulers upriver of Freetown, the capital of Sierra Leone, teamed up with one Curtis, a European slave dealer, in a challenge to the British anti-slave-trade campaign. The British response was the Rio Pongo expedition. A force that included recently arrived WIR troops travelled up the Rio Pongo and punished Curtis and his local chief allies, establishing a procedure that was followed over subsequent decades. Hence, in 1823–24 another expeditionary force that included WIR troops was led by Sir Charles McCarthy, the governor of Sierra Leone and of the British West African holdings, to meet a challenge from the king of the ancient and powerful Ashanti (Asante) people in the Gold Coast (now Ghana).

The Ashanti king considered the British to be trespassers on his coastal territories. His army was well organized and well led, and his warriors were brave. For the British the outcome of the Ashanti expedition was mixed. In 1823 the Ashanti defeated a mixed force that included the Second WIR, and early in 1824 they laid siege to Cape Coast Castle, the seat of British government. Governor McCarthy, most of his staff and a fair number of WIR troops were killed in the fighting. This emboldened the Ashanti and they

The Second West India Regiment in Barbados, 1880. Photo by W.D. Cribbs. (Brian Dyde, *The Empty Sleeve: The Story of the West India Regiments of the British Army* [St John's, Antigua: Hansib Caribbean, 1997].)

engaged the British in skirmishes for the rest of the 1820s. The situation ended with a Treaty of Amity and Commerce in 1831. This treaty, which failed to address the issue of Ashanti versus British sovereignty over the southern Gold Coast, maintained an uneasy peace into the 1860s, when war broke out again.

In the meantime, a similar situation erupted in the Gambia in 1831 and required the same type of expedition; a military outpost, Fort Bullen, was seized by a Mandingo force and had to be recaptured. In 1840, after almost two decades of fighting in the jungles and rivers of the Upper and Lower Guinea region, the designation of the Third WIR (the unit that had originally borne this title had been disbanded in 1825) was conferred on the locally raised troops. This unit was tasked with garrisoning and defending all the British settlements in West Africa.

Meanwhile, the rest of the WIRs were based in the Caribbean. It was agreed that units would alternate between the

The West India Regiment in Jamaica, 1898. Note Sergeant Gordon, VC, on the extreme left. Photo by W.D. Cribbs. (Brian Dyde, *The Empty Sleeve: The Story of the West India Regiments of the British Army* [St John's, Antigua: Hansib Caribbean, 1997].)

two sides of the Atlantic, with two companies from the First, Second and Third WIR serving in West Africa while others were stationed in the Caribbean islands or the mainland colonies. As their comrades in Africa marched and fought in dank jungles, troops in the Western Hemisphere adjusted to the monotony of garrison duties. The region was not entirely quiet, however, for its stability was threatened by occasional acts of disorder. For example, in 1816 there was a slave uprising in Barbados (the Bussa revolt) and in British Guiana, and in 1831 a major uprising in Jamaica took place. In both instances WIR soldiers were instrumental in restoring order, though in 1837 they themselves were the cause of trouble. More than three hundred men of the First WIR, stationed at that time in Trinidad, mutinied. They were all conscripts, and they wanted to return to their homes in Africa. Though they were able to arm themselves and burn to the ground the hutted encampment in which they lived, they were overcome without difficulty and their ringleaders hanged.

The West India Regiment in action in Sierra Leone, 1894. W.D. Cribbs. (Brian Dyde, *The Empty Sleeve: The Story of the West India Regiments of the British Army* [St John's, Antigua: Hansib Caribbean, 1997].)

In Africa the work of pacification went on as one local chieftain after another made resentful gestures against the spreading influence of Britain. New colonies were established – in 1850 the Gold Coast became separate from Sierra Leone – but the troubles of this region continued to follow a familiar pattern. In the Gambia the Marabouts, a sect of Muslim extremists, declared a jihad, or holy war, against unbelievers that threatened not only British prestige but also neighbouring African tribes, who asked for protection. A punitive force from the First, Second and Third WIR, together with local militia, marched on the sect's capital at Sabaje in 1852. After shelling the town they captured its huge and fanatically defended mosque and destroyed it. In the Gold Coast a revolt among coastal groups such as the Fante and Ga, caused by the taxation system, was crushed and the seat of government was rescued from siege.

The WIR troops had hardly completed their missions in the Gambia and the Gold Coast when they were called into action in the Malagia expedition, in the region of the Mellacourie and Scarries rivers in Sierra Leone, in 1854 and 1855. The expedition's artillery and rockets enabled them to create a satisfactory blaze as they set fire to the settlement and withdrew in boats. However, the flames went out; ordered by an officer to go ashore the following day and finish the job, they walked into vicious opposition from an enemy that had had all night to prepare. The West Indians fought with desperate bravery but were driven into the river with heavy losses; few were able to swim to safety.

Their next major engagement was the Badibu war in Gambia in 1861 against the Mandingo chieftain of Sabra. The arrival of the WIR with heavy firepower provided the usual show of strength, but once the troops were ashore they were charged by a fierce native army that included three hundred cavalry. The men immediately adopted the classic European battlefield tactic of forming squares, which, just as at Waterloo, prevented the horsemen from inflicting heavy casualties. Their nerve and discipline held, and they drove off the enemy.

By now the West Indian troops had gained considerable skill in this type of operation. Using small forces, often of 150 men, they were extremely adept at marching in the jungle, bombarding fortified positions and storming enemy stockades. They carried out classic assaults of this kind at Sabra and Madonkia, routing their Muslim opponents. They were able to develop and improve these skills because the WIR's constituent units spent long periods in West Africa – the tour of duty was four years (later reduced to three), with the different regiments serving in rotation.

The soldiers who stayed in the Caribbean experienced a good deal of boredom under the "Pax Britannica", so much so that virtually the entire Second WIR volunteered to serve in the Crimea when war broke out between Britain and Russia in 1853. The offer was declined by the War Office, but, though West Indian soldiers did not fight in the conflict, the war did have an important and lasting effect on them: their uniform was redesigned as a result of the impressive appearance of the French army's Zouaves, who were serving alongside British troops in the Crimea.

Zouaves were originally recruited in French North Africa in the 1830s, though gradually units of French soldiers also adopted their distinctive costume. A dandified, unmilitary and seemingly impractical uniform, it consisted of voluminous trousers, gaiters, a short embroidered jacket and a turban or tasselled cap. It was extremely colourful and, worn with suitable rakishness, very impressive. British soldiers were fascinated by it and it was later copied by regiments serving on both sides in the American Civil War. In 1855, when Queen Victoria made a state visit to Paris, she too was taken with the uniform, making several drawings of it in her sketchbook. It is thought that from that time she wanted some unit of her own troops to be similarly dressed. She did not have long to wait: the Gold Coast Corps was outfitted in this style within a year. Shortly afterward the West India regiments were also ordered to wear the uniform. With its baggy dark blue trousers, white spats and scarlet jacket, it became the badge of identity for West Indian soldiers until the disbandment of their units in the 1920s. The Zouave uniform is still worn in their memory by bandsmen in the Barbados Defence Force.

Peacekeeping

The 1860s were difficult years in the West Indies. The Civil War
in America meant a dramatic fall in sugar prices and a sharp
increase in the cost of imported foods. The result was ruination.
In Jamaica, on the advice of the island's draconian governor, a
petition to Queen Victoria from poor blacks asking for assistance
received an offhand response. Their misery increased, and rioting
broke out in October 1865 at Morant Bay, where the courthouse
was burned down and several whites were killed. Governor Eyre
reacted by placing the island under martial law and savagely pun-
ishing any blacks whom he considered to have taken part in the
riots. There followed several days of further rioting before the so-
called rebellion was put down by magistrates and the militia, with
a good deal of severity. The rebels' perceived figurehead, a planter
named George Gordon, was hanged, though an official enquiry
later exonerated him. The island was placed under direct rule
as a Crown Colony, thus ending the growing influence of small
planters and some coloureds in the legislature.

The Morant Bay insurrection aroused controversy throughout the Empire and is now considered one of the key events in
Jamaican history. Its result was a bloodbath in which members
of the First and Sixth WIR were actively involved, destroying
houses, making arrests and executing people who were often
innocent and who could, in addition, be their friends or relatives. The official regimental history later commended their
faithfulness in performing these duties, though Eyre's handling
of the crisis provoked outrage – and a governmental enquiry
– in England.

Of a less controversial nature was the WIR's service in
Central America, where it was sent to counter a threat from
hostile native Indians as part of the British Honduras Field
Force. The soldiers established a number of outposts in remote
areas, one of which was Orange Walk, in the northern province of British Honduras. There, on Sunday, 1 September 1872,
without warning 180 Mayan Indians descended on the small

WIR detachment with the aim of destroying the garrison and town centre. The Mayans mounted several attacks and maintained a heavy fire but they were eventually beaten back. The courage of Sergeant Belazario and Lieutenant Smith saved the day as they secured and distributed vital ammunition to their comrades at a critical period in the battle. Three WIR soldiers were awarded the Distinguished Conduct Medal, and one of them, Sergeant Belazario, came within a whisker of winning the Victoria Cross.

Africa Again

While WIR soldiers were winning laurels in the Western Hemisphere, their old adversaries in Africa were being as troublesome as ever. Both the Ashanti and the Marabouts continued to threaten British territory or interests and were dealt with in the usual way. In June 1866 an expedition sent to destroy a stockade at Tubab Kolon (Tubabecelong), near the River Gambia, included a young

The storming of Tubab Kolon, the Gambia. Painting by Chevalier Louis W. Desanges from the Penzance and District Museum and Art Gallery. (Brian Dyde, *The Empty Sleeve: The Story of the West India Regiments of the British Army* [St John's, Antigua: Hansib Caribbean, 1997].)

soldier born in Tortola named Samuel Hodge, who won the Victoria Cross.

The troops bombarded the stockade without either knocking it down or chasing off the defenders, so a party went ashore and set about it with axes. They hacked at the wood while under intense close-range fire, and Hodge had just managed to sever the gate fastenings when he was hit and badly wounded. As he fell his comrades forced open the gate and flooded in. Hodge died some months later in British Honduras. He was the first black soldier to be awarded Britain's highest military honour. (See appendix B for a list of West Indian holders of the Victoria Cross.)

The war against the Ashanti continued. The WIR had more experience of fighting the enemy in this environment than any other unit in the British Army. When in 1873 a punitive force – made up largely of white soldiers – set out for the enemy capital under the command of Sir Garnet Wolseley, the WIR marched with it. They found themselves filling a logistical role, carrying supplies for the rest of the expedition, because they were both more acclimatized than European troops and more disciplined than native porters would have been. Nevertheless, they earned the battle honour "Ashantee 1873–74". And this was not their only glimpse of glory; two men were awarded the Distinguished Conduct Medal for a courageous scouting mission.

The security of West Africa depended in large measure on these men, who continually proved their worth. They fought and defeated recalcitrant tribes whose names – Yoni, Sofas, Mende – are lost to history but who were skilled and formidable enemies. They deserved the battle honour "West Africa 1887", which recognized their long commitment to the region. They also won a second Victoria Cross, in March 1892, that marked the heroism of a Jamaican, Lance-Corporal William Gordon. He was part of an expedition in the Gambia in 1891 to apprehend Fodi Kabba, a recalcitrant tribal leader. The pursuit led, as ever, to a defended stockade. While the British officer in charge was supervising a battering-ram to knock down the gates, snipers began firing at close range from loopholes in the walls. Noticing that one of the enemy weapons was aimed at the officer, Gordon flung himself at his superior, knocking him to the ground and thus saving his life while under fire.

The effectiveness of the West Indians in this corner of the Empire that they had so thoroughly made their own is reflected in a tribute paid after yet another expedition – in 1894 – against a rebel tribe:

> Thus ended the [Ijebu Yoruba] campaign. In five days a force of several thousand men had been routed, a walled town of four miles in circumference, containing a population of at least 15,000 had been captured, and a thickly-populated territory of 8,000 square miles had been brought under the influence of the British flag. All this had been accomplished by a force of little over four hundred troops, led by sixteen Europeans.[1]

The WIR's old enemy, the Ashanti, were finally subdued during the 1890s. They lost their struggle to assert their independence when Britain annexed their territory in 1902. The bitterest fighting experienced by the West Indians in this part of Africa, however, was against the followers of the charismatic rebel leader Bai Bureh, who became the focus for resistance to a hut tax demanded by

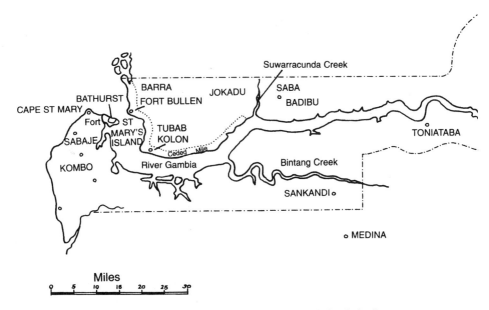

The Gambia. (Brian Dyde, *The Empty Sleeve: The Story of the West India Regiments of the British Army* [St John's, Antigua: Hansib Caribbean, 1997].)

the British in the hinterland of Sierra Leone. He was eventually captured by other troops, but the WIR received yet another battle honour: "Sierra Leone 1898–99". A year later West Indian troops captured Sankandi in the Gambia, in what was to be the last of the numerous colonial campaigns they fought in West Africa.

At that time some of their comrades were seeing a different form of service, guarding Boer prisoners of war on the island of St Helena. The Boer (South African) War was a humiliating experience for Britain. Soldiers were in such short supply that, for the first time, members of militia units and "volunteers for the duration" were allowed to serve overseas alongside professional soldiers. Because of the Boers' racial attitudes, however, it was thought inadvisable for black troops to fight in a "white man's war", and WIR soldiers were given garrison duty. Their presence horrified the Boer prisoners. A similar attitude was shown by St Helena's white population, and it is to the credit of those men that they fulfilled their duty unflinchingly in such a hostile situation.

A military and economic backwater, the Caribbean would languish until the opening of the Panama Canal, in 1914, gave it new strategic importance by placing its islands on a major sea lane from the Atlantic to the Pacific. With slave rebellions no more than a memory, there was little for soldiers to do. By the end of the nineteenth century European garrisons had been reduced to a fraction of their former size or removed altogether (British troops were withdrawn from Barbados and St Lucia in 1905), and members of the militias idled through their period of service without seeing action of any sort.

Sugar continued to decline, or, rather, it was taken over by corporations – largely American – that bought up land, closed down mills and transferred the processing of cane to factories. This transformation from an industry based on individual plantations to one centred on large processing plants created unemployment and increased the poverty and hopelessness that was by now characteristic of much of the Caribbean. Proposals were made for the diversification of agriculture, and enquiries (Royal Commissions) were held to study alternatives. One crop – bananas – resulted from this process when an American company introduced them at the end of the century, but growing and shipping small quantities of diverse crops was simply not considered economical.

Education also languished and literacy rates were extremely low. In a largely agricultural society it was not considered important to provide education beyond a basic level. The mother country, after all, would provide the personnel to run a colony's churches, legal system and administration, while government was best left to the professionals of the Colonial Office, whose governors often brought with them years of experience ruling similar territories elsewhere.

Though the British Colonial Service had extremely high standards of probity and efficiency, its approach could only add to the frustration felt by indigenous populations. Large numbers of them were able to find a worthwhile future only by migrating to work in North, South or Central America. At the beginning of the twentieth century the excavation of the Panama Canal proved a source of employment for West Indian labourers, who were able to send remittances home, but this situation ended with the canal's completion shortly before the First World War.

PART 2

The Impact of the First and Second World Wars

CHAPTER 9
The First World War, 1914–1918

Eleven battalions of the British West Indies Regiment were also raised and some were sent to France, East Africa, Mesopotamia and Egypt.

The outbreak of war in August 1914 was greeted in the Caribbean with a patriotic fervour that gladdened the hearts of jingoists. On the outbreak of war Barbados (and other islands) claimed to have sent to London encouraging telegrams urging, "Go on Britain: Barbados is right behind you." The colonies – as represented by their press, legislative bodies and public meetings – overwhelmingly supported Britain in a conflict that was unlikely to impinge on their own region. In large measure the colonies expressed their loyalty by fundraising, with the different islands competing to produce the largest sums. Contributions were, however, frequently in commodities rather than in money. The islands could donate sugar, of course, and rum, which was extensively used by both the navy and the army. (It was gulped down, for instance, by many thousands of infantrymen minutes before they left their trenches to attack the Germans on the Western Front.) Raw materials such as arrowroot and cottonwood were also sent and, in at least one instance, locally harvested cocoa was made into chocolate and shipped to the troops in decorative tins that bore a message typifying the spirit of the times: "The Gift of the Colonies of Trinidad, Grenada & St Lucia to His Majesty's Naval & Military Forces. This chocolate is made from cocoa grown in Trinidad, Grenada & St Lucia." More impressively, the islands also paid for nine aircraft for the naval and army air services.

The British West Indies Regiment on the Western Front, September 1916.
(Imperial War Museum Q1202.)

Why was there this enthusiasm, given the remoteness of the
conflict and the fact that its major issue – German aggression –
was of no relevance to the West Indies? Years of indoctrination
had led the people of the region to view themselves as part of the
British Empire and to take a degree of pride in membership in this
"family". The war – a more significant event than any West Indian
had yet experienced – presented the image of the mother country
in peril, the economic, political and social system with which they
had grown up threatened by a largely unknown and aggressive
European power. The reality of this threat, reinforced by a relent-
lessly patriotic press, was sufficient for many to set aside – at least
temporarily – peacetime preoccupations with poverty. Domestic
political considerations were expected to be quickly shelved "for
the duration". Interestingly, the same was true in other parts
of the Empire; in Ireland, for instance, where civil war between
Protestants and Catholics had been expected to break out at any
moment, the two sides postponed their quarrel (at least until
Easter 1916). In Britain itself, the suffragettes' civil disobedience
campaign to win the vote was similarly put in abeyance until the
return of peace. Though this feeling was not to last in the West
Indies, it gave some impetus to the colonies' war effort.

For some idealists the war presented an opportunity to advance the cause – by demonstrating their worth – of coloured people. It enabled colonial subjects to prove their loyalty to the Empire, to show patriotism, ability and self-sacrifice equal to that of the British, and to impress the white establishment. In much the same way women earned the right to vote through the wartime jobs they carried out. The *Federalist* in Barbados – traditionally the most conservatively "British" of the islands – made this point in an editorial:

> As coloured people we will be fighting . . . to prove to Great Britain that we are not so vastly inferior to the Whites that we should not be put on a level, at least, of political equality with them. We will be fighting to prove that the distinction between God-made creatures of one empire because of skin, colour or complexion differences, should no longer exist, and that some opportunities should be afforded the Coloured subjects of the empire as fall by right of race to its citizens. We will be fighting to prove that we are no longer merely subjects, but citizens – citizens of a world empire whose watch-word should be Liberty, Equality and Brotherhood.[1]

Despite competition among islands to demonstrate enthusiasm for the British cause, these idealists also imagined that the war would create a common sense of identity. Another publication, the *West Indian* newspaper in Grenada, advised that the people of the region

> should first learn to cultivate the spirit of regionality; to look beyond their cocoa fields and cane fields into the broader outlook of West Indian interests. The war that is being waged in Europe today affords to the world a great object-lesson in Unity and Self-Sacrifice. Let us hope that West Indians, as represented in these scattered islands of the Caribbean, will have long abandoned their mutual suspicions, prejudice and reservations of pride, and be quite prepared to enter into [a] spirit of oneness of purpose . . .[2]

There was not, however, a rush to enlist, as there was in Britain or in the white dominions. The conflict was too far away and the number of potential recruits too small for the War Office in London to immediately raise new West Indian units. When Britain declared war on Germany on 4 August 1914, the conflict was expected to be, as the oft-repeated phrase had it, "over by Christmas". There would be no time to train recruits in a distant part of the Empire and transport them across the Atlantic. There seemed no point in bringing such soldiers to a thoroughly unfamiliar environment to fight an enemy that would undoubtedly be better trained and better acclimatized than they were. Britain possessed the world's largest navy, which was expected to play the major role in defending the British Isles and the colonies. There was also an excellent but small regular army and a territorial force. With the outbreak of war, government policy was that Territorials should be sent to take over garrison duty in India and other colonies in order to release regular units for service in Europe. In addition, several overseas territories – Canada, Australia and especially India – had their own regiments of regular soldiers that could be dispatched to the conflict immediately. In all of these places, however, there were also volunteers for military service, and they would be accepted for service before the War Office needed to consider West Indians as soldiers.

Race was undoubtedly a significant factor. At home there had always been suspicion on the part of a small but influential white interest towards the notion of arming blacks en masse. This element felt that training large numbers of them in the use of weapons could be storing up trouble for the future, that their loyalty could not be relied upon and that to transport them, at great expense, to other parts of the world might give them dangerous political ideas. It was argued too that the islands could not afford to lose a significant proportion of their manpower without affecting the production of raw materials essential to the war effort. There was also the issue of blacks killing whites – at the time a concept that was unacceptable to international public opinion.

Though volunteers came from the colonies to support the mother country, the colonies themselves were – by tacit international understanding – supposed to be neutral territory in the event of war. In practice this notion was ignored by both sides. British and imperial troops, including the WIR, at once invaded Germany's

African possessions in Togo, Cameroon and South West Africa. In Tanganyika, on the other side of the continent, German forces put up a much fiercer resistance. African-German troops fought against white, coloured and black Allied forces. While both sides fielded black units in this fighting, the belligerents were reluctant to use them in Europe. The Germans' often harsh treatment of their own black colonial subjects was well-known throughout the world. Though professional Indian troops were used in France and Flanders from early in the war, it was only gradually, as the losses of European manpower became more severe, that the Allies began to send colonial troops into the trenches of the Western Front. The first to do so were the French, who brought in their North African troops as they had done half a century earlier in the Franco-Prussian War.

Clearly, in these circumstances West Indians had little opportunity to volunteer for war service, or incentive to do so, even though the conflict did briefly impinge on their region. There was a real threat from German raiders in the Western Hemisphere. At the start of hostilities a squadron of German warships commanded by Admiral Graf von Spee had been at sea. Unable to return to their home port, they ranged through the Pacific and the southern Atlantic, creating alarm out of all proportion to their numbers. This force did not reach the Caribbean; it was hunted down and sunk off the Falkland Islands in December 1914, though only after it had destroyed a British naval force off Coronel, in Chile. However, another warship did: *Karlsruhe,* operating in West Indian waters, sank sixteen British merchant vessels over a three-month period. It was neither captured nor sunk, but was destroyed by an internal explosion. These German raids provided a sharp reminder that no coastal region of the globe could be considered beyond the reach of a hostile navy. By the end of 1914, however, the German naval threat to the area had been removed and the West Indies were no longer in danger.

The War Office initially argued that West Indian soldiers were needed for the defence of their own islands. As the war widened it was urged that they should be sent to Egypt to fight the Turks or used to garrison the West African territories captured from

Germany. The War Office proved indecisive, and both it and the Colonial Office insisted that the matter should be resolved by the other. Public opinion in the Caribbean was growing increasingly restive, however, demanding to know why the services of its young men were being rejected. King George V, who favoured the West Indians, prodded the War Office into action, and the secretary of state for war, Lord Kitchener, agreed to the raising of a West Indies contingent in addition to the already existing WIR. The *London Gazette* announced that "His Majesty the King has been graciously pleased to approve the foundation of a corps from Contingents of the inhabitants of the West India Islands, to be entitled the 'British West Indies Regiment (BWIR)' ".[3]

Recruiting for this new force began in the autumn of 1915. The first batch of men, from Jamaica and British Honduras, set off for the United Kingdom a few months later. Others who made their own way occasionally experienced a cool reception. The *Stratford Express* reported from West Ham Police Court:

> Nine black men, natives of Barbadoes, West Indies, were charged with being stowaways on the S.S. Danube. Mr J.W. Richards, who prosecuted for the Royal Mail Steam Packet Company, said that the S.S. Danube made a voyage from Trinidad to England, and the day after leaving Trinidad the ship called at Barbadoes. It was presumed that the men came aboard there for the day. Afterwards they were found on the vessel. Mr Gillespie: In a dark corner, I suppose? (Laughter). Mr Richards continued that the men were put to work, and they did not cause any trouble. He was told that the men were desirous of enlisting in the Army. Mr Gillespie: What, do they want to enlist in the Black Guards? (Laughter). Det. Sgt Holby said he had made enquiries at the local recruiting office and they told him they could not enlist because of their colour, but if application was made to the War Office no doubt they could enlist in some regiment of black men. Remanded for a week.[4]

Standards were high at the recruiting stations. As well as the stringent levels of health and fitness required, candidates were chosen only if they were likely to be a credit to the colony from which they came – it was to be seen as a privilege to serve. Both the rejected and the successful soon had important grievances, however. They had given up their livelihoods to enlist, and in many cases those who were turned down could not return to their former occupations. Recruits selected in some islands had to wait for the lengthy periods necessary for assembling the contingents. Boredom and frustration understandably began to afflict them, and fever spread through the camps.

New Faces

On arrival in England, the new recruits were quartered in temporary camps at Seaford in Sussex and Withnoe near Plymouth. They were greeted by an intrigued British public with excitement, curiosity and warmth – but the welcome was to be their only experience of warmth. They had arrived in the midst of a British winter, and many fell ill at once. Their camps were not properly heated and frostbite claimed a number of casualties, as did measles.

A similar fate befell the third contingent, which left Jamaica in March 1916. It sailed north to Halifax to cross the North Atlantic, but by the time their unheated ship reached Nova Scotia more than six hundred men had frostbite. Five died and more than a hundred had to have amputations. The victims of what came to be known as the "Halifax incident" were returned to Jamaica three months later as invalids, only to find that the pensions to which they were entitled had been delayed. The matter was extensively covered in the local press and caused such an uproar that recruiting had to be suspended.

By this time, in any case, volunteering for war service had lost some of its appeal. After two years of fighting there seemed no prospect that Germany would be defeated soon. There was also no disguising the reverses – such as the Gallipoli campaign – that the Allies had suffered. A significant number of young men saw no point in volunteering for service overseas.

No coloured West Indian could at that time become an officer; the highest rank he could achieve was warrant officer. Educated blacks therefore faced limited options while qualified whites could expect to be commissioned more or less automatically. Private soldiers, used to the lackadaisical West Indian lifestyle, in which speed and punctuality were not considered necessary, found it immensely difficult to adapt to military discipline. Their natural reaction was to answer back, and this added greatly to their problems. Many men, having gone barefoot all their lives, could not get used to marching in boots, hobbling along painfully on route marches. Judges and magistrates passing sentence on petty criminals began to give them the option of military service instead of prison. While this filled the ranks, it meant that a lower standard of black recruit began to join the contingents. In a deliberate effort to foster regional cohesion, men from several colonies had been mixed together in the BWIR, but instead of creating *esprit de corps* it led to fights between the groups. There were also clashes between soldiers and local police in Trinidad and Jamaica.

Eleven battalions of the BWIR were raised, which were split between several fronts. A total of 397 officers and 15,204 other ranks served in the regiment.

Table 9.1: Number of Serving Men per Colony

Colony	Men
Jamaica	10,280
Trinidad and Tobago	1,478
Barbados	831
Bahamas	441
British Honduras	533
Grenada	445
British Guiana	700
Leeward Islands	229
St Lucia	359
St Vincent	305
Total	15,601

Source: Channel 4, "Black and Asian History Map", http://www.channel4/history/microsites/B/ blackhistorymap/

Two battalions went to France and one unit was sent to East Africa, where the climate was affecting white troops. Another hundred went to Mesopotamia as part of the Indian Expeditionary Force, but the main force was posted to Egypt, where the strategically vital Suez Canal was threatened by the Turks. In none of these theatres were they initially expected to do any fighting. Non-white soldiers saw little combat and in the main were assigned to the task of carrying ammunition. Although they were in uniform and had military training, they were treated by the authorities as labour units, akin to the coolies of the Chinese Labour Corps. They suffered the same horrors of war as white troops but did not have the same status. This was greatly resented by the West Indians, and when reports of the situation began to appear in the press at home, enthusiasm for the war was further diminished. The BWIR units, however, began to be increasingly used in combat.

At Basra, in Mesopotamia, West Indians skilled in boat handling were used to good effect in transporting troops and supplies, but it was the units in the Egypt Expeditionary Force (EEF) that made the most useful contribution to the war. In November 1916 a conference in Cairo decided that, owing to continuing shortages of men, the West Indians would be used in combat. The threat of Turkish invasion was acute and all members of the EEF were trained extensively in attack and defence. The West Indians were at last given an opportunity to show their mettle. When fighting began, the BWIR became involved in one of the war's most decisive and successful campaigns: General Allenby's offensive in Palestine, in which they pursued the Turks across the Sinai Desert, through the Jordan Valley and into Syria.

The West Indian troops in Palestine earned the praise of those who commanded them. The commander of a machine gun company to which some of them were attached commented: "The men worked exceedingly well, displaying the qualifications necessary for a machine-gun section, viz. a keen interest in their work, cheerfulness, coolness under fire, an intelligent application of what was required of them and the necessary ability to carry it out under difficulties." Referring to a specific incident, he continued:

"Although they were only issued with Vickers guns a few days before the raid, their immediate action was excellent and they were able to keep their guns in action during a severe test."[5]

Other senior officers recorded their satisfaction with the performance of West Indian troops. The commander of the corps to which they belonged stated: "The Second Battalion, British West Indies Regiment . . . has shown an excellent spirit. The soldierly bearing and smart turn-out of the battalion have been maintained under the most trying circumstances, and . . . this is most creditable to all ranks."[6]

Major-General Sir E.W. Chaytor, who commanded Australian and New Zealand troops in Palestine, sent this message to the regiment: "You showed great keenness in reconnaissance . . . your conduct left nothing to be desired, and all through every report I have had has been most favourable. Indeed, all the troops of my division report that they like to fight alongside you; in fact, they could never wish for anybody better."[7] He went on: "The bearing of these two battalions was excellent throughout. In the trenches their discipline was of a high standard, and great enterprise was displayed by their patrols. They displayed great steadfastness under fire and dash in the attack, and gave proof of marching power of a high order."[8]

Tribute was also paid to the West Indians who served in East Africa. An officer who observed them wrote:

When the conditions seemed most hopeless, they never seemed to give in, and the saving grace of humour seemed always to be present. On a patrol, when everyone had to sleep in pouring rain, when too tired to march any further, the only comment was: "Serve me right for me fastness to join Contingent. When I get home I will be 'fraid even to join a church."[9]

These testimonials were praise indeed, but they were to be the BWIR's only reward. Though the battalions in the Middle East had proved they could fight as well as any imperial troops, the War Office had already decided that all further contingents arriving from the Caribbean would be sent as labourers to the Western Front. In April 1917 one colony, Jamaica, had introduced conscription, and the flow of men was now steady. What these recruits found on reaching England or the battlefronts was boredom, frustration and discrimination. As before, many arrived ill, or quickly became so in the unfamiliar climate. They were housed in primitive camps and subjected to military discipline, but had no effective outlet for their energies. Though they regarded themselves as a cut above the Indian and Chinese labourers, they were acutely aware of discrimination from the British soldiers, who often sneered at and taunted them. They were excluded from a pay increase given to other Empire troops, and were often barred from using recreation facilities available to the rest of the army.

Aftermath

At the end of the conflict the battalions of the BWIR were reunited at Taranto, in southern Italy. Part of the regiment had been there for some time, loading supplies that were sent on to the Allied forces in Salonika, Mesopotamia and Egypt. Now they were all confined in a camp and being used as dockworkers. Many of them had had no leave since enlisting as much as three years earlier, and with the war over they saw white troops being demobilized and sent home ahead of them. By the beginning of December 1918 they had had enough – a mutiny broke out.

The trouble lasted four days and had to be put down by British troops. The men refused to work and there were attacks on officers (their demands included the removal of white officers, though no coloured ones were available to replace them). All the indignities that West Indian soldiers felt they had suffered over the war years found expression in this mutiny. Moreover, their rebellion was not unique. Canadian soldiers at a camp in Scotland also rioted because they were not being sent home fast enough. Many white troops from the Empire felt belittled by the haughty attitude of the British.

A significant outcome of the incident at Taranto was the formation of a discussion group, a nascent political organization called the Caribbean Forum. One of its leading members was Clennel

Wickham, from Barbados, who wrote in the press about his experience. Nowhere were the grievances of black troops more fervently discussed than in the sergeants' messes, in which could be found the most educated and politically aware of the black soldiers. Though they were able to do nothing more than talk, the members formulated many ideas about the future of their region, the social and political rights of blacks and the possibilities for unification of the British Caribbean territories. Taranto proved to be a sort of political university for a generation of West Indian intellectuals, and it influenced the thinking of many servicemen once they returned home.

The ugly mood that had sparked the Taranto mutiny continued throughout the following year as shiploads of West Indian servicemen were repatriated. They continued to resent the treatment they had received and to agitate for the pay increase that they were still being denied. Many had spent time in England prior to sailing for the Caribbean, and there they had experienced an unpleasant upsurge in racial violence. With the conflict over and unemployment now a major problem, the British did not want foreigners of any sort taking work from their own people. There was also, as there had been during the war, resentment at the perceived success of black men with local women. The West Indians whose arrival as wartime allies had intrigued the British population were often now taunted and attacked in British ports and cities; as always, these incidents were reported in the newspapers at home.

By the summer of 1919, when the largest number of BWIR veterans sailed for the Caribbean, very little was left of the loyalty to Empire that had been evident at the outbreak of war. The atmosphere aboard some of the repatriation vessels was frequently menacing to other passengers and crew. When a ship brought Jamaican soldiers home they found a crowd gathered to welcome them, but also a British warship standing by in case of trouble. The authorities were fully aware of the climate of feeling created by the war, but they could not decide whether to treat the men as returning heroes or as potential insurgents. For this reason the founding of any ex-servicemen's organization was viewed with suspicion.

"Contingent men" took part in several riots in Jamaica, Trinidad and British Honduras. Often these gatherings were spontaneous, but some were deliberately planned, resulting in mayhem. At the same time, veterans turned their backs on the official acts of remembrance for those who died in the war, refusing, for instance, to march in ceremonies at war memorials or on anniversaries. They were, nevertheless, eventually granted the long-withheld army pay owed to them. The salient characteristics of their wartime experience, however – the sense of alienation and rejection by the Empire's white Establishment, the sense that their contribution was neither wanted nor valued and the imputation that any white man, no matter how worthless, was of more importance than the most able black – were to prove the Caribbean's real and lasting legacy from the First World War.

Disenchantment

The WIR had also emerged from the war with a sense of disenchantment. Because both Germany and the Allies had extensive colonies in Africa, it had been a foregone conclusion that the continent would be involved in the fighting. The West Indians had the most extensive experience of bush warfare of any unit on either side, yet they had been overlooked, at least to begin with. Members had served in both East and West Africa, but in the latter – the conquest of the German colonies of Togo and Cameroon – no more than two hundred were deployed, as signallers and machine-gunners, in a mixed force of colonial troops.

Over five hundred men of the WIR had been sent to the altogether more rigorous theatre of East Africa. Here the brilliant German commander Paul von Lettow-Vorbeck, realizing that he had no hope of defeating Allied forces with the few men and resources at his disposal, had decided instead to tie down as much enemy manpower as possible to take pressure off German armies elsewhere. He succeeded brilliantly, and kept up his guerrilla campaign until November 1918. His technique was to stay on the move and to mount endless nuisance actions but to avoid pitched battle. Against this background the WIR soldiers had served in an Allied mixed-bag force with Indian, African and Arab troops, and were awarded eight Distinguished Conduct Medals and six Military Medals.

The end of the war found WIR troops guarding a supply depot in the Middle East. They remained in that region until they returned to the Caribbean in the middle of 1919, bringing with them their battle honours: "Cameroons 1914–16", "East Africa 1914–18" and "Palestine 1917–18". But the WIR was not destined to survive for long in the postwar world. With great armies demobilizing everywhere, there was no obvious reason for the existence of a regiment whose home was in a comparatively tranquil corner of the world, nor did Africa offer them further prospects of campaigning or peacekeeping. Moreover there was no influential lobby to agitate for its survival. In 1920 the regiment was reduced to a single battalion (a far cry from the twelve regiments raised 130 years earlier) and six years later orders were received that it was to be disbanded entirely. The regiment paraded for the last time at Up Park Camp in Kingston in 1927, and shortly afterwards a brief ceremony, attended by a small number of officers, was held in London in the presence of King George V. The colours were laid up in Windsor Castle, where they joined those of other disbanded units.

CHAPTER 10
The Interwar Years, 1919–1939

Poverty and lack of opportunity in the West Indies greet returning troops.

While David Lloyd George, Britain's prime minister at the end of the First World War, talked of making his country "a land fit for heroes to live in", no one could pretend that much of a future awaited the servicemen who returned to the Caribbean. Poverty and lack of opportunity made the region – in an equally memorable phrase of Lloyd George's – "the slums of the Empire". Sugar still dominated the economy, though in Trinidad there was now also oil, but wages were low in both industries, and agriculture – apart from harvests of tobacco, coffee and fruit – offered even more limited prospects. Seasonal workers were idle for much of the time, and when jobs were available they often had to be shared; men in Trinidad worked on average four days a week, while on other islands it was often only two or three. Alternatively, men might be employed full-time for two weeks and then dismissed so that others could replace them for a similar period.

With this poverty came a sense of hopelessness. Education for most was rudimentary, and those who did succeed in getting through secondary school had few opportunities for a useful career. The civil service was dominated by white British officials, though this could be to the benefit of the territory (the greatest strength of the colonial civil service was that its members had no family, commercial or political ties to the areas they administered, and were thus impartial). Demands for "localization" of posts began to be heard. For local people, university or a job in Britain was virtually undreamed of, and not even the army offered a career once the WIR had been disbanded. Labourers had no unions to provide mutual support or articulate their grievances, so their only means of venting frustration was to riot.

The worldwide depression that began on Wall Street in 1929 reduced the West Indies to even greater misery, and the second half of the 1930s was marked by an increase in social and industrial disorder. In 1935 there was an outbreak of labour unrest on the sugar plantations of British Guiana and a sugar strike in St Kitts. There was a strike in St Lucia and in St Vincent a violent protest against an increase in customs duties. Two years later there were sugar strikes in Jamaica and St Lucia, and the following year saw the most serious instance of strife: the Jamaica dock strike in which nearly thirty people died and more than a hundred were injured. In the space of a few short years the Caribbean had become a hotbed of militancy. Both trade unions and political parties sprang up virtually overnight; the Caribbean's most famous party, Jamaica's People's National Party, dates from this time. In 1938 a labour congress convened in British Guiana expressed a series of demands that resonated throughout the region: federation of the colonies; the expansion of elementary education; health insurance; old age pensions; universal suffrage; and a legislature entirely elected by the populace rather than appointed by Government House. The final demand was for nationalization of the sugar industry. But these were only hopeful resolutions; there was no question of any government's putting them into effect.

Unrest

In response to threats of disorder, colonial governors asked for troops to be sent to the region. Assistance would arrive in the form of sailors and Royal Marines from a British warship, as when HMS *Exeter* was sent to Jamaica to quell rioting. These young military men had minimal training and equipment, and no knowledge of local conditions. One of them later recalled his experiences:

Towards the middle of May, 1938, whilst taking part in a practice "shoot" with *Exeter*, we were dispatched at full speed to
Jamaica, at the request of the Governor, as serious rioting had
broken out in the Island, led by a left-wing labour leader named
Bustamante – later to become the Island's Prime Minister.

Shortly after our arrival in Kingston, the Island's capital,
having already been detailed off for the Seamen's Platoon, I found
myself being drilled in the art of dealing with civil riot, practice
being carried out in a large shed alongside the jetty belonging
to the Fyffes Banana Co. A few days later the Seamen's Platoon
and R.M. Detachment were ordered to go ashore and proceed
into the centre of the town where serious rioting had broken
out. All we, in the Seamen's Platoon, were equipped with in
the way of weapons were entrenching-tool handles, which were
a sort of long hammer shaft, whilst the Lieutenant in charge
was equipped with a revolver. We were marched into the town
centre where a mob of some 200–300 Blacks had overturned
streetcars, smashed shop windows and had started looting. We
were lined up across the street facing the mob who were armed
with pitchforks, iron bars, stones and an assortment of other
weapons. It was a rather frightening experience for a lad of 18,
facing this screaming, shouting mob.

The Lieutenant in charge called over his loud-hailer for order,
and ordered the mob to disperse. The appeal was to no avail,
and shouting and making threatening gestures towards us, they
continued to advance. The situation was getting ugly and the
Lieutenant again ordered them to disperse over his loud-hailer.
When they refused to move, he drew his revolver and fired two
shots over the heads of the crowd. This tended to pull them up
with a round turn, and in the meantime, the Royal Marines who
had been infiltrated quietly in small groups in the side streets,
now moved forward so that the mob in the main street were
now surrounded by armed Royal Marines. They now moved in,
breaking up the crowd into small groups, and moving them on
forcibly. This seemed to do the trick, and gradually the crowd
began to disperse and drift away. We hung around long enough
to ensure that there would be no more violent demonstrations
that day, and were finally marched back to the ship. No one had
been seriously hurt, and we had, by our very presence, turned

what might have been a very serious situation into a reasonably peaceful one. After all, we had no personal animosity towards the population.[1]

The young sailor observed at first hand the hardship that was responsible for this type of disturbance, for his ship was berthed alongside the wharves where locals waited – often in vain – for work.

The Jamaicans are normally a happy-go-lucky type of people, and as far as I could gather, the riots were the result of a very bad unemployment situation (far worse than in Britain), very low wages, long hours, and unsanitary housing conditions. On the banana wharf alongside the ship, for instance, a long line of Jamaican men, women and older children would line up from early morning. [The line] used to stretch from the end of the wharf, round and through the banana sheds, and down into the holds of Fyffe's ships that were being loaded. Three or four of the workers would, on getting to the head of the queue in the sheds, pick up a long stalk of bananas, hoist them on their shoulders and move towards the doors. On passing through the doors facing the ship to be loaded, a heavily-built Black with a machete would, with deadly accuracy, slice the stalks between each of the carriers into smaller bunches, whereupon the worker would carry them down into the hold of the ship and stow them. On returning topside, the worker would receive a disc from the Company's representative which they would later exchange for 1 shilling from the Company Office at the end of the wharf. If they queued all day for between 8 and 10 hours, they might be lucky to earn between 2 and 3 shillings, if they were exceptionally patient. Inevitably, many of the women and young girls drifted into a life of prostitution in the numerous bars and cabarets that surrounded the dock area, and venereal disease was very rife.[2]

As a result of these continuing events, a major enquiry – the Moyne Commission – was set up during that year to investigate social and economic conditions. But it was too late. There was no time to study these matters in depth or to formulate solutions before the Second World War broke out, and all questions of reform had to be postponed.

CHAPTER 11
The Outbreak of the Second World War: The Home Front

Many West Indians volunteer for service in the United Kingdom and help to finance the war effort. Meanwhile, more American troops pour into the Caribbean as the area becomes a hotbed of war activity.

For every subject of King George VI, the Second World War began with this announcement from Britain's prime minister, Neville Chamberlain, which was broadcast by the BBC on Sunday, 3 September 1939:

> I am speaking to you from the Cabinet Room of Number 10 Downing Street. This morning the British Ambassador handed the German Government a note stating that, unless they withdrew their troops from Poland by 11.00 a.m. a state of war exists between us. I have to tell you now that no such undertaking has been received and, consequently, this country is at war with Germany.

After years of well-intentioned but fruitless attempts to restrain, by diplomacy and by concession, the increasingly aggressive policies of Adolf Hitler, the German dictator, and his Italian ally Benito Mussolini, Great Britain had at last, in early 1939, committed itself to the defence of Poland in the event of its being attacked by Germany. France also declared war on Germany, and the whole European continent was now in crisis – even neutral nations would be gravely affected by coming events.

But this was not solely a European crisis. British subjects living in Africa, India, the Far East and the Caribbean were also involved. The largest segments of Britain's overseas empire (now the Commonwealth) swiftly declared war on Germany on their own behalf. India, Australia and New Zealand did so on the same day as Britain. South Africa followed on 5 September and Canada on 10 September. Eire (formerly the Irish Free State), which was in the process of severing its ties to Britain, opted out and remained neutral for the duration of the conflict. The rest of the old Empire – the colonies – voted to support Britain's declaration of hostilities.

In Barbados the acting governor issued a proclamation that was typical of those posted throughout the West Indies:

Notice of the Existence of a State of War

Whereas a state of war has arisen between Great Britain and Germany as from the third day of September one thousand nine hundred and thirty-nine, it is hereby proclaimed that such state of war applies also to this Island as from the aforementioned third day of September one thousand nine hundred and thirty-nine.

Given under my hand and the Great Seal of the Island of Barbados at Bridgetown . . .

GOD SAVE THE KING

A youth living in Grenada had reason to remember the moment that the news reached his island – he was given the task of broadcasting it. An article described how "Cosmos Cape . . . recalls earning 6 pence or 9 pence for ringing the bell all day long at the Roman Catholic Church in Grenville, to announce the start of the war. He remembers it as the second wage he earned as a young man."[1]

The outbreak of war had a major effect on the overseas British territories. The Empire was run from London, and any change in the situation there was bound to have an impact on the colonies. The United Kingdom was their biggest trading partner and the market for their raw materials. It was the home of their head of state and of the Colonial Office, which provided their administration. It was also a place of overwhelming sentimental importance to the different colonial peoples, even though the great majority had never been there. The English (or Scottish) established Church, British sports, British education using British textbooks, the royal family, the cult of empire as presented in the British media – all created a powerful image of this worldwide community as a single, interdependent entity. Although Australians and East Africans might have little interest in each other, the mystique of empire ensured that they all felt part of the same community.

Though this level of feeling is difficult to imagine today, it was then an extremely potent force. It was very noticeable in the Caribbean, as witnessed by a number of accounts. Randolph Beresford of British Guiana recalled:

> The colonies were more British than the British. We celebrated the King's birthday. Every child from the school, from all the schools in the town, met and parade [*sic*] to an area where there's a bandstand and sing "God Save the King". We were told – we understood – we were a part of Britain, we were British. We weren't anything else.[2]

Another commentator perhaps took this feeling to extremes:

> I held England in very great esteem. I read every book about England I could lay my hands on. I knew almost everything about England, every coalfield and steelworks, their size and description. All our geography in school was based entirely on England. Whilst one knew very little about West Indian history, one's brain was full of knowledge where English history was concerned. We were always told – and we always had this thing at the back of our minds – that England was the Mother Country. So we held her in the highest regard and this was shown in patriotism.[3]

Similarly, a Jamaican expressed a view that was widespread: "Since Great Britain was in a war I felt like it was my duty to take part in helping to gain a victory for Her, for ourselves and for the world."[4]

For people in Britain, the war began with air-raid warnings. For their counterparts in the Caribbean there was also danger, though of a different nature:

NOTICE
4th September 1939

It is notified for general information that at about 6.30 p.m.
yesterday three submarines were sighted off the north-east coast
of St Kitts. The nationality of these vessels is unknown. In view
of this and reports of the presence of enemy submarines in their
waters originating from the USA stations which were broadcasting yesterday, the public are asked to co-operate with the
Authorities by reporting immediately the presence of any suspi-
cious craft which may be seen around the coast.[5]

Though Britain and the European conflict obviously seemed
close in spirit, they were not unimaginably distant in physical terms either. In the winter of 1939, in fact, the war seemed
uncomfortably close. As we have seen, Britain's first major naval
engagements of the previous war had taken place in the Western
Hemisphere, where a squadron of German ships commanded by
Admiral Graf von Spee had defeated and sunk a Royal Navy
force off the coast of Chile. London had dispatched more and
better ships to hunt them down, and a month later, in December

The German battleship *Graf Spee*. (Bermuda Maritime Museum.)

1914, von Spee and his squadron were themselves sunk off the Falkland Islands.

Now history, after a fashion, was repeating itself. The Royal Navy's first success in the new war also took place off the coast of South America. In December 1939 a German battleship – ironically named *Graf Spee* – was brought to battle by the British cruisers *Ajax*, *Achilles* and *Exeter* in the battle of the River Plate. The German vessel, badly damaged, put in to the harbour of Montevideo in Uruguay. Unable to make a break for the open sea, the ship was scuttled and its captain, Langsdorff, committed suicide.

This event was a major talking-point in the Caribbean. It had proved that the enemy could appear anywhere in the region and that no place was safe. While large surface ships such as *Graf Spee* were rare and conspicuous, British naval experts were aware that Germany's U-boats could reach stealthily into distant seas and strike without warning. For this reason the entire Caribbean had to take seriously the issues of defending the coasts, blacking out lights and guarding against spies and saboteurs. The people of these lands were to share the risks and the fears of people in Europe, even if they were to be spared the trauma of occupation by German troops.

Officially West Indian waters were neutral: on 2 October 1939 the United States government had proclaimed a "Pan-American Neutrality Zone" that was intended to keep the war from entering the Western Hemisphere. An invisible line running due south from Halifax, Nova Scotia, to a point north-east of the Leeward Islands, then zigzagging south-east and south-west to skirt the bulging Brazilian coastline, sealed off the neutral United States and the republics of Central and South America from action by Germany. The concept was unworkable in practice because there were territories in this region that belonged to belligerent countries, and they quickly became a valuable source of raw materials. They were not only important but also inadequately defended, and it was therefore likely that they would be targeted.

In the first flurry of activity after war broke out, the islands' local defence units were brought up to strength. This gave a practical outlet for the patriotic feelings of local men, although they were not destined to play any important role in events. A St Lucian described his service in one of these units:

When World War Two was declared on September 3rd 1939, I answered the call to arms in response to the bugler's call around town. I had been a member of the St Lucia Volunteer Defence Force from 1936. During the intervening period, war had raged between Ethiopia and Italy and there were rumours of impending war in Europe.

We were put through the rigours, drills, practices and tactics: skirmishes, machine guns, and infantry, all in preparation for the defence of the Island. We were under the command of Captain T.G. Wade (of the Prince of Wales Volunteers) and his senior subaltern Lieutenant Mercier [was] a veteran of the First World War. They were assisted by Lieutenants Pink, Swaby, Devaux and Haynes, Sergeants Caraneth, Baird, Captain Theobalds and Major Lambert, commander of the local forces. We were two platoons of thirty rank and file and also received training from Royal Marines.

By ten a.m. every active member of the Volunteer Defence force was present at the muster. Full mobilization was declared and we were then pressed into active service. The Quartermaster issued all the appropriate supplies, blankets, helmets, water bottles etc. At inspection there was great excitement! What a sight, everyone saddled from man to beast.

Guards were posted at Government House, the lighthouse, the electric power station, the Customs [House] and wharf, the batteries at Point Seraphine, Point Victor, wireless station, cable hut and all places thought necessary for defence. Most dreadful of all was the watch on the tugboat "Midge" of Public Works and the dredger at the harbour mouth. We realized of course that full active service had begun.

Government offices and business firms lost some of their clerks engaged in the Corps until relief was officially granted. Many craftsmen were also members of the Corps. The police were assigned separate duties. Our camp was set up at the Military Hospital at Vigie because our Headquarters at the drill hall alongside the Police Headquarters and in front of the prisons proved inadequate.

Within weeks we were made comfortable at Vigie along the lines of orderly army routine and discipline. The King's Regulations and Army Act were enforced, with an Orderly Room for offenders. There were cooks and galley, sickbay, and transportation was a major consideration. The sound of the bugle regimented our lives.

All went well until the local Treasury and Army Headquarters could no longer continue financing our mobilization.

Though his unit was reduced to a token force, this soldier was able to list other local units that survived until the end of the war:

There was also recruitment and enrolment of men and women for a Windward Island Contingent. There was an Auxiliary Territorial Service [ATS] group with its rank and file being drawn from Guiana, Trinidad, Grenada, Antigua, St Vincent, Barbados, St Lucia, Dominica, and some personnel from the UK. The company remained active until the end of the war and several of its troops were decorated for their service. There was another naval group, the Trinidad Naval Volunteers and Merchant Seamen.[6]

The Home Front

All this was made possible when in 1942, after the United States entered the war, all local forces in the British Caribbean were taken under Imperial Command. These men and women were required only for home defence, however, and initially there was no thought of involving them in service abroad. In 1939, as in 1914, the dominions were able to help the war effort quickly by sending troops, because all of them had existing regular army units. Britain, which had introduced conscription in 1938, built up its armed forces with impressive speed. For the most part, however, in the colonies there was no move to do so. The government in London made it clear that the most vital issue was Britain's need for raw materials and that the best contribution overseas territories could make would be to keep on producing and supplying them. Lack of manpower to carry out this task could slow down the war effort.

At the beginning of 1940, Whitehall informed colonial governors that they should dissuade members of their communities from volunteering for military service, and instead encourage them to remain in their peacetime jobs to increase the output of local resources. East African cotton was badly needed, as was mahogany from British Honduras (it was used for making aeroplane propellers) and petroleum and pitch from Trinidad. It was to be emphasized that this unexciting work was the best way of helping the war effort.

The secretary of state for the colonies was quoted as saying, "Foodstuffs and minerals . . . are no less potent instruments than munitions in modern warfare. It [is] the duty of the Colonies to increase production so as to be as independent of imports as possible and to have as much as possible to export." And a pamphlet titled *How the Colonies Can Help to Win the War* explained:

> The most important thing that every man, woman and child in the Colonial Empire can do to help the War Effort is to save. As much as possible must be produced and sold to the Allies and to foreign countries; purchases from foreign countries must be cut down drastically; and no more must be bought even from Britain than is absolutely imperative and urgent. If we produce more and consume less, there will be a margin for saving. This should be lent to the Government. The British Government is spending at the rate of more than £8,000,000 a day.
>
> We can all help to foot this tremendous bill, by saving up to the very limit of our power. But we shall not be pulling our full weight until we have cut down our spending (especially on imported goods) to the bone. That is the contribution everyone can make.[7]

Jill Hamilton, who was a child when the war began, remembered the impact of new realities on the eating habits of Barbadians:

> We began to grow far more foodstuffs than we had done previously. I recall a large bed of onions in the kitchen garden. One afternoon I went out with my parents and the gardener for a pow-wow as to whether the crop was ready. It was decided it

should remain for another week. What a sad decision because within a couple of days the onions had been reaped by thieves.

Also imported was rice, a staple starch for our population, which came from British Guiana. For that commodity, as well as for kerosene, ration cards and coupons were issued to all the inhabitants of the island.

The then Director of Agriculture, Dr John Saint, activated a scheme where Barbadians were educated to eat what we grew and to grow what we ate. Estate owners were instructed how many acres of every food crop they were to cultivate and private owners could also ask for advice. It was Dr Saint who undoubtedly saved this little island from starvation. On his advice sweet potatoes were adopted as the substitute for the scarcer imported rice.

We were fortunate at home as we reared all varieties of animals, ranging from a cow, through sheep, pigs, ducks, chickens and pigeons. Rabbits were also bred and they were a great source of food for the table. Mum compiled "Wartime Recipes for use In the West Indies" by Mrs St J Hodson. She put her expertise into book form and sold it in aid of war funds.

Jill Hamilton also mentioned another significant wartime change:

One of the precautions taken throughout the island was a black-out of all buildings, especially those visible from the sea, and all lights of vehicles. Yards and yards and yards of black material were purchased and draped over windows and doors and if that didn't stop the light creeping through then plywood was bought and nailed onto the offending areas.[8]

The control of panic and rumour was of great importance to the war effort. The Government of Antigua issued this notice to all telephone subscribers in July 1940:

1. Don't repeat war rumours on the telephone, or discuss them in any way.

2. If any one tells you the latest rumour, ask him where he got the information. You will probably find that he cannot or will not tell you.

3. Don't try to repeat news bulletins, even British Official News Bulletins, on the telephone, or ask anyone else to do it for you.

It is almost impossible to do so correctly without a written copy. You are almost certain to make a mistake, and this is one way of starting rumours.

4. Do all you can at all times to check the spread of Rumours. They never do any good and may help the enemy.

5. Put this where every one can see it who uses the telephone.[9]

The most vital thing that the Caribbean could send to Britain was oil, of which Venezuela and Trinidad were important suppliers. Oil produced there was transported the short distance to refineries on the Dutch islands of Aruba and Sint Maarten (St Martin). Venezuela's oil supplemented that of Trinidad, which was the largest source of oil in the British Empire at that time. It was also the site of the Empire's largest refinery. From Trinidad, Venezuela, Aruba and Curaçao oil was shipped in tankers north to the United States and across the Atlantic. Trinidad's Gulf of Paria thus became for a few years one of the world's most important assembly points for merchant shipping convoys, and its capital one of the world's busiest ports.

The region also exported bauxite, which was used to make aluminium, an essential for aircraft manufacture. The traditional Caribbean export, sugar, was of course as much in demand as ever. Otherwise the islands concentrated on achieving self-sufficiency in food provision to avoid tying up British shipping. The type of intensive farming seen all over the British Isles began to be practised in the West Indies. As a government leaflet observed regarding one island, "By increasing her own food crops, Jamaica has cut down her imports considerably and this [has] made an important contribution to the war effort."

The colonies gave money. While Britain was holding off the Germans it needed all the financial support it was offered. Colonial and dominion governments made substantial loans to the British Treasury or waived repayment of old debts. At an individual level, people in the overseas territories were vigorously encouraged to open government savings accounts that would make their money available to loan to the British war effort.

Table 11.1: Monetary Donations to Britain from the Colonies During the Second World War

West Indies	Gifts (£)
Bahamas	125,200
Barbados	202,332
Bermuda	344,133
British Guiana	128,877
British Honduras	26,590
Jamaica	223,376
Leeward Islands	37,262
Trinidad	929,095
Windward Islands	58,338
Total	2,075,203

Other Colonies	Gifts (£)
Aden	77,454
Ceylon	1,096,101
Cyprus	13,424
Falkland Islands	71,656
Fiji	169,321
Gambia	11,478
Gibraltar	58,172
Gold Coast	361,696
Hong Kong	399,731
Kenya	386,032
Malta	35,193
Federated Malay States	5,963,744
Unfederated Malay States	1,151,411
Straits Settlements	9,479,475
Mauritius	301,962
Nigeria	409,255
North Borneo	37,649
Northern Rhodesia	409,942
Nyasaland	164,214
Palestine	38,832
Sarawak	316,380
St Helena	5,681
Seychelles	15,762

Table 11.1 cont'd

Other Colonies	Gifts (£)
Sierra Leone	148,698
Somaliland	7,574
Tanganyika Territory	420,988
Uganda	302,118
Western Pacific	45,032
Zanzibar	40,770
Total	21,939,745
Grand Total	24,014,948

Note: This list includes only monetary gifts that were brought to the notice of the secretary of state, and not monetary gifts made directly to organizations in the United Kingdom or gifts in kind.

Source: His Majesty's Stationery Office, *The Colonial Empire (1939–47)*, appendix 2 (London: His Majesty's Stationery Office, 1947), 115.

In addition there were numerous campaigns to buy things for the British populace. The Germans first bombed London in the summer of 1940, and in the following month their sustained bombing campaign against British cities – the Blitz – began in earnest. Pictures of the destruction, the wounded and the homeless created a wave of sympathy throughout the world. Many Caribbean islands and colonies donated mobile canteens – vehicles that could be driven to stricken areas to dispense meals and drinks – something that could be truly appreciated only by those who had just spent the night in an air-raid shelter.

Typical of these campaigns were two that were described by the Antigua Broadcasting Service. They indicate that children too played a significant role in raising funds, and that the causes to which their efforts were devoted were sometimes unusual.

3rd May 1942
Antigua Warships Fortnight

The latest news of Antigua Warships fortnight is that although hampered by some six inches of rain in the last five days, contributions are coming in well.

Over £8 was collected at the A.C.C. grounds last Sunday afternoon when the Band of the Antigua Defence Force rendered musical items. HMS *Antigua* made her appearance on Wednesday morning and was given a rousing welcome. Her visit lasted from about 10 a.m. until nearly noon and no less than £34 was collected in the streets of St John's. The Boy Scouts and Girl Guides had very bad luck in their fete on Thursday 30th. Rain fell nearly all day and certainly affected the success of their effort. We are glad to state that the collections received so far total £1,370.

24th Feb 1943

The Children's Fete held at the High School on Thursday was most successful. They made, after paying expenses, more than £25.

The Fete was organized completely by some third term girls, varying in age from 10 to 13. These were: Gwen Peters, Fred Peters, Pamela Thompson, Melba Thompson, Norah Thomas, Jacquie Winter and Jean Harrison. They were helped by three girls from the Fourth Form – Gathia Terry, Cicely Thomas and Marjorie Moore. So the age of the Organizers and Stall Holders varied from 10 to 14.

Some of their school friends from different forms ran some of the Side Shows for them and also played the piano for the Dancing. Mr Burrows lent his cart and horse, and the children very much enjoyed the drive. Most of the needlework on the Stall was done by the Stall Holders who have been working hard to make and collect things for their Fete.

The proceeds are to be sent to the Fund in England for providing milk, as well as other food, for the starving children in Greece.[10]

Another useful and popular gift was that of recreation huts. These were basic, easy-to-assemble buildings that, like the mobile canteens, provided meals and drinks. For British servicemen and women the war involved a great deal of lonely and uncomfortable duty, such as fire-watching on rooftops, walking cliff-top beats as sentries guarding the coasts and manning anti-aircraft batteries in remote locations. It made a world of difference to the morale of these troops to have a warm, dry and cheerful place to which they could go when off duty. Inside there was usually a sign that would say, for instance, "Given by the people of St Kitts" to remind them whom they had to thank for this comfort.

Even more useful was the fact that territories could buy and donate aircraft. Uganda – a much bigger and wealthier territory than any in the Caribbean – paid for a whole squadron of Hurricanes. Jamaica also made a significant contribution, sending more than £80,000 towards the cost of a squadron of bombers. The result, 139 "Jamaica" Squadron, was one of the first to be equipped with the highly effective Mosquito aircraft, and saw service throughout the war. Trinidad similarly outfitted a fighter squadron, number 74.

> I left Trinidad in November 1941 to Britain to join the RAF. My squadron was called the Jamaica Squadron, not because we were Jamaicans but because the people of Jamaica had raised the money to buy the planes we flew. The pilots and navigators were from all over – Poles, Norwegians, another Trinidadian and a crazy Dutchman who had escaped Occupied Holland to join the RAF.[11]

Prisoners of War in Jamaica

Traffic between the West Indies and Britain was not, incidentally, all one way. Connie Mark recalled the arrival of German prisoners of war, who joined interned enemy nationals in confinement at Up Park Camp outside Kingston:

> At Up Park Camp we had a prisoner of war camp and when war was declared all the German and Italian seamen in the area were taken off to internment. I worked at the hospital and if they were sick they had to come there for treatment. And we had a special corps that guarded them. They were called the Pioneer Corps. We had a lot of Germans in Jamaica because about 150 years ago a whole village in Germany emigrated to Jamaica, around Seaford Town and St Elizabeth. Most of the people they had guarding them were German-Jamaicans from Seaford Town.
>
> They got out a lot because they built a new officers' mess and a new sergeants' mess there, and worked as gardeners and cooks in the officers' or warrant officers' quarters. So although

they were POWs [prisoners of war] they weren't locked up. The Germans and Italians have a lot of talent so they used to make a lot of leather goods, and maybe twice a year, they'd sell their wares that they made. And I remember I bought a lovely leather writing case. We used to buy things that they made. And another man was very proficient: he made dolls' furniture. He must have been a carpenter or something in Germany. I remember I bought a whole drawing room and bedroom suite for my niece made by the German internee.[12]

Refugees from Gibraltar

There were also refugees, most famously perhaps a group of civilians from Gibraltar. Gibraltar was a naval base that controlled the entrance to the Mediterranean and was therefore strategically vital. Three miles long and one mile wide, it was a city as well as a fortress, and with the coming of war its people faced considerable danger of attack from Mussolini's Italy or from the Spanish, whom Hitler attempted to gain as an ally. In 1939 and 1940 there was a significant threat of invasion, and heavy air raids. The British government decided to evacuate much of the civilian population, who were sent to London.

When the British capital itself became the target of concentrated air raids, which began in earnest in September 1940, it was decided that the Gibraltarians must be moved again. There were thirteen thousand of them, too large a number to be accommodated anywhere else in Britain. It was also feared that these men, women and children, who were used to a balmy Mediterranean climate, would suffer widespread illness in the unaccustomed damp of an English winter. It was decided to send them across the Atlantic to other British territories; after a good deal of discussion, the governments of three Caribbean islands agreed to accept them. The Gibraltarians themselves knew nothing about their destination until they were officially informed by this announcement:

To the people of Gibraltar in London:
His Majesty's Government greatly regret that it has been

necessary for you to leave your homes in Gibraltar on account of the threat of enemy action, and they have given very careful consideration to the arrangements which should be made for your safety and welfare. It is their desire and intention that you and your children should be able to live comfortably and safely for the remainder of the war under conditions as similar as possible to those to which you have been accustomed in Gibraltar.

These conditions are unfortunately not available in England where damage from enemy action will persist, the winter is damp and cold, and the accommodation available is limited. But in the British West Indies the Governments of Trinidad, Jamaica and St Lucia have generously offered to provide temporary homes for you while the war lasts. Some of you may be reluctant to undertake another journey, but in the West Indies the climate is warm and sunny like the climate of Gibraltar; suitable accommodation with greater privacy for each family can be provided and facilities will be available for the education of your children. His Majesty's Government are fully satisfied that it will be in your interests to go to the West Indies and that you will be assured of a warm welcome from the people of the loyal British Colonies to which you are sent.[13]

In the event, the evacuees in England did not go to the West Indies, and only one island played host to other Gibraltarians. The Atlantic Ocean had been made perilous by enemy U-boats – in September 1942 U-48 sank the *City of Benares*, which was carrying four hundred passengers, including children, to safety in Canada. After that incident the authorities became more cautious about sending civilians overseas. Nevertheless, a second contingent, numbering sixteen hundred, was shipped directly from Gibraltar to the Caribbean.

Their destination was Jamaica, and in Kingston the Public Works Department was obliged to assemble in frantic haste a camp to accommodate them. This was set up on the Mona Estate, a short distance outside the city. Designated Camp Number 1 because others were expected quickly, it was not only built but also provided with lighting and a water supply in the space of one month. It is a matter of record that local contractors and a local labour force made valiant efforts to have everything ready in time for the arrival of their guests. When the Gibraltarians landed, a large crowd greeted them and lined the road to their new home. A song, "Welcome Gibraltar", was even composed in their honour.

The camp was organized with a great deal of thought. It consisted of wooden huts 150 feet long, divided lengthways by corridors with fourteen rooms on each side; these rooms could house either two or three people. All were furnished, and all the rooms had access to verandahs that ran the length of each building. Families were able to live together, and as much as possible former neighbours were housed in the same building. The Jewish community, a group of less than forty, was also able to live together. Meals were taken in communal dining halls, of which there were three: one for adults, one for children under fourteen and one for mothers with infants or babies. All the cooking was done – at least initially – by Jamaicans, who did their best to learn and provide dishes with which the evacuees were familiar.

There were numerous other facilities. A "canteen" sold groceries, clothing, sweets and basic medicines. There was a post office, a bank and a small hospital that was also equipped to provide dental care. There were recreation halls and a sports ground, and a school in which education followed the Gibraltar syllabus. Jesuit priests – an order especially favoured by Gibraltarian Catholics – provided spiritual guidance. The camp's inmates took advantage of these opportunities, establishing their own sports teams, choir, amateur dramatics society and Boy Scout and Girl Guide troops. In addition to these home-grown diversions, regular concerts were provided by local military bands. The camp also had a police station and was protected by a twenty-strong police detachment made up largely of Jamaican officers. Since the Gibraltarians were unaccustomed to the notion of black policemen, four of their own men were appointed special constables and added to the force.

Though the camp sounds like a great improvement on the dangerous conditions in which they lived at home, it was not long before discontent surfaced among the Gibraltarians. The establishment was run by a four-man committee comprising a commandant (a professional colonial civil servant), a deputy (the camp manager), a food controller and a Catholic priest. A very long list of rules had been drawn up before the camp was occupied, and these were strictly enforced by the commandant, who had wide powers over the camp's population. For instance, though the visitors were welcome to visit any part of the island and coaches were provided to transport them into Kingston, no inmate was allowed to leave the camp – which was surrounded by a wire fence – without written permission from the commandant. Nor were local people allowed in, except under strictly regulated conditions. In order to avoid causing resentment in nearby communities by competing for jobs, evacuees were forbidden to look for work outside the camp.

The commandant thus had the power to control the lives and movements of those inside. He could dictate mealtimes and demand roll-calls; he could provide modestly paid jobs within the camp – and take them away as punishment. He had the right to levy fines for breaches of the rules and, in extreme cases, could order individuals to be detained in cells at the police station. He could also take action against locals who entered the camp without authorization to sell goods. A number of them who had been expelled joined in the mounting criticism of the camp government. The most visible symbol of authority – the police – came in for a good deal of abuse from within and without.

As the months passed a groundswell of resentment developed. The people in the camps were, after all, not refugees, let alone criminals. They had had the misfortune to live in a dangerous corner of Europe. They had paid for this by being removed from all that was familiar to them and sent to another hemisphere, to an environment in which they felt deprived of basic freedoms. Boredom became a real enemy for people whose energies had previously been absorbed in running households, earning a living and making their own lives. An anonymous spokesman was quoted in the local press:

> We all like Jamaica and we deeply appreciate the great kindness and sympathy we are receiving from outside the Camp, but we do feel that having been brought here under military exigencies, thereby depriving us of homes and means of livelihood, we should be treated as responsible human beings, and not mere nuisances to provide a living for a few petty officials.[14]

And the newspaper's editorial accurately guessed the reason for the increasing number of complaints against camp discipline:

> Everything seems to have been provided for our evacuee visitors, except something to do. A human being, particularly a female human being, must have some occupation in order to keep his or her mind in a state of normal health; and yet the very daily occupations which form the background of a woman's existence, housekeeping, washing, cooking, have been taken away from our visitors, who have highly qualified chefs, to cook for them; a scientific (and expensive) laundry to wash for them. All they really need now is a valet service to dress them. One of the worst hardships you could place these people under would be to leave them with nothing to do, no interest in their daily lives.[15]

There were cases of outright, though small-scale, rebellion: people defied a regulation against taking food out of a dining hall, and gathered noisily outside the police station when a woman was confined there – for no more than a few hours – for unruly conduct. Letters from inmates to their relatives overseas expressed bitterness about the strictness of the regime and voiced outrage at incidents of mistreatment. These turned out, after official investigation, to be almost entirely exaggerated or based on hearsay.

Discontent within the camp was a talking-point outside, and a local newspaper attempted to understand both sides:

> We wonder how many people comprehend the great difficulty of the job that these gentlemen have undertaken. The evacuees are decent, self-respecting persons who are in no sense of the word under any kind of stigma; yet it is clear that hundreds of persons, moved bodily into a new country, under strange conditions and in what is really a foreign environment, must for their own protection be subjected to a certain amount of benevolent discipline. To keep order among a large population, to inspire contentment and satisfaction among people removed from their normal surroundings, to feed, to cater for the bodily, mental and spiritual needs of such a body, is no easy task. If the public understand the problem, we feel sure that they will

extend that co-operation which is so necessary if the right spirit is to be created. Our visitors are welcome guests, who have been brought to a place of safety, where all possible is being done for their welfare.[16]

The issue of discontent was never settled, and many Gibraltarians spent an unhappy interlude on the island, though this was not in any way the fault of their hosts, who had gone to great lengths to make them welcome. The occupants of Camp Number 1 were the only members of their community to be sent to the West Indies during the war (their quarters, also known as Gibraltar Camp, later became the temporary home of the University of the West Indies). The evacuees who had gone to the United Kingdom, and whose departure had been delayed by the Battle of the Atlantic, remained in Britain until the end of hostilities, and no attempt was made to settle evacuees in Trinidad. With the Allied invasion of Europe in June 1944, the war against Hitler had clearly begun its final phase, and within a few months the Gibraltarians were able to return home. They departed from Kingston on 24 October 1944.

Naturally this was not one of the war's more exciting events. Nevertheless, it was highly important to a small group of people who would otherwise have had to live in danger, either at home in Gibraltar or in London. With the passage of time and the fading of grievances, Gibraltarians have since come to feel gratitude to the people of Jamaica for their kindness and hospitality.

Despite being a safe haven for evacuees, the Caribbean was not a quiet corner of the war, and it became even less so after the United States entered the conflict in December 1941. There were now two major enemies – the Axis powers (Germany and Italy) and Japan – and the two theatres of war were linked by the Panama Canal, which became even more strategically important than it had been. In addition, US ports on the Gulf of Mexico, which also shipped oil to Britain, enhanced the region's wartime value. The Pan-American Neutrality Zone ceased to be recognized as soon as the United States became a belligerent.

Anti-submarine patrol in the Caribbean off the Panama Canal. (Imperial War Museum, NY6121.)

Since 1939 the United States had been actively fortifying the Canal Zone, and now it turned its attention to the islands that guarded its approaches. The United States had already (in 1917) bought the Danish Virgin Islands because of their strategic importance. Now the process was taken further through a deal between President Roosevelt and Prime Minister Churchill in 1940, when Britain's fortunes in the war were at their lowest point. In exchange for the use of fifty elderly US Navy destroyers – essential for escorting convoys of merchant ships – the United States was granted permission to establish bases on eight British transatlantic

A house-an-hour building programme, Trinidad. (*National Geographic,* June 1942.)

territories, including six in the Caribbean. After the United States entered the war in December 1941, construction of these bases and fortifying of the Caribbean territories were carried out with remarkable speed and intensity.

Throughout 1942 a massive programme of site clearing, building and occupation took place, an experience that was to change forever the character of these island communities. Antigua, the Bahamas, St Lucia, Jamaica, Trinidad and British Guiana all received American garrisons, as did the Dutch Antilles and the US's own territories of Puerto Rico, the Virgin Islands and Cuba's Guantanamo Bay. This massive construction programme provided a number of the territories with the roads, airports and seaports that form a necessary part of the infrastructure of modern nations. A book published by the United States government in 1943 – while the work of defence-building was still going on – sums up the importance of the region and the hum of activity:

Look at the map and see those island stepping-stones that curve in the shape of a bow enclosing the Caribbean Sea that, in its

turn, guards the Panama Canal, the short-cut route between
the Atlantic and the Pacific Oceans. Look at Antigua, just
about in the middle of the island stepping-stones. Then think
of the importance stepping-stones have in the world today for
submarines and airplanes.

Since the first boatload of American army engineers arrived
at St John's, the emerald island of Antigua has resounded with
unaccustomed activity. There have been the noise of enormous
dredging machines and the sound of American voices. First
came the engineers to get things ready for the soldiers: barracks
had to be built and made comfortable; the dredgers had to get
busy to make an airfield; and many other preparations had to
be made to meet the demands of the American soldiers. All this
had been taking place at Parham Harbor on the northeastern
side of the island, only five miles from St John's. But when you
consider that Antigua is only twelve miles long, you will realize
that distances between places are not very great, and that the
whole island is within easy reach.[17]

The same publication described work at the southern end of the
island chain:

The United States sent Americans down to Trinidad for a special
job. They were to turn that island into the strongest fortress of
all the Caribees.

The construction of these camps, naval bases and airfields
was a fast project. Through the heart of deep woods American
engineers had to hack their way, and with them went surveyors
to plan out the area that must be levelled and turned into a
town of barracks, aviation fields, and supply stores. Thousands
of workers, black and white, Negro and East Indian, had to
clear huge areas before construction crews could do their work.
At the same time, down at the harbour of Port of Spain, thousands more workers had to build a naval base for seaplanes and
enlarge the berth for ships. When it is all finished, there will still
be about fifteen or twenty thousand American soldiers stationed
there to garrison this powerful fortress that guards the southern
approaches to the Caribbean Sea.[18]

CHAPTER 12
Service Overseas

Tasks for the armed forces, merchant navy and the civil population.

While the Caribbean was a theatre of war, what of those from the region who sought to contribute to the war effort and serve the Crown by travelling to other theatres? Not all who volunteered for war work were motivated by patriotism. The colonies were desperately poor, and unemployment had been particularly high throughout the 1930s. Thus for many the prospect of paid work outweighed any dangers and disadvantages – and there were both in profusion.

One possibility was to join the Merchant Navy and sail in the very tankers and freighters that the U-boats were hunting. For reasons that were all too obvious, there was a constant need for crew members. Large numbers of West Indians were driven by poverty to endure the stress of transatlantic voyages in return for relatively good wages. During the early part of the war there can have been few more hazardous jobs than crewing those vessels. It meant long days and nights on the stormy Atlantic or the Caribbean, knowing that at some point German submarines would be lying in wait, and that at any moment, especially at night, the first indication of their presence would be a torpedo striking the hull. Many of the colonials who served aboard these ships were Indians called lascars, but there were a good many West Indians too. White sailors were paid much more than colonials – £24 a week as opposed to £6 15s – and had better accommodation. Only the risks they ran were the same. At least those who died received equal commemoration; the Merchant Navy Memorial at Tower Green in London records the names of fifteen hundred colonials alongside those of their white shipmates.

A freighter torpedoed by a U-boat. (Imperial War Museum, HU40216.)

Another possibility was to work in Britain, and some West Indians were very keen to do this. Athelstan Holden, a Jamaican, made this charming comment on his motives: "I had this feeling that I could better myself in England – although I did not know how or why. I told myself that England is a country of great learning, and some of it is bound to rub off on me. All I had to do was get there."[1] Another West Indian wrote:

> My memory is of a large placard somewhere: "Do you want to help the war cause?" it read. "England needs you." England, that great country, needs me. Of course it had a terrific psychological effect. It didn't say that you had to have so many Junior or Senior Cambridge certificates. They only wanted you – not your qualifications. It didn't even say that you had to be fit – just "Do you want to serve England, your Mother Country?" and it continued: "At this moment England is in dire trouble and so England needs you."[2]

Like Mary Seacole, many of the first volunteers for wartime work in Britain paid their own way; others had their fares paid by generous public subscriptions.

Some men – 520 to be exact – were given work in munitions factories, where they were able to earn the same rates as whites. Initially several young men were selected to train for this work in England, and one of them described how they were recruited. He was one of a group of Barbadians who were summoned by official letter to appear at the Labour Office in Bridgetown.

> The Labour Officer invited us into the Queen's Park House and bade us to be seated, then he mounted the rostrum and gave a speech. The gist of what he said was as follows: The Mother Country was at war, and that there was a dire need to defeat the Nazis' forces. He went on to say that we were a group of fine young men and we were invited to go to England to help in the struggle. We were not being asked to go as soldiers, there were enough of them already, but the soldiers needed the tools of war with which to fight; things like guns and planes and tanks. What was needed were engineers to make these instruments of war. He said: "You are a fine group of men and you were chosen to go to England to train as engineers. First you will go to college to learn how to make instruments of war, then you will go into the factories and help to make them. If you prove to be successful then others will be invited to follow suit."

Another official then "handed out pencils and sheets of paper, saying, 'I want you to write an essay on 'Why you want to go to England'. While we were busy writing, he wrote five arithmetic problems on a blackboard . . ." These tests completed, the candidates were dismissed, but a fortnight later the young man was told he was going. At the same time, more recruits had been sought through an advertisement in the newspaper:

> The crux of the matter was that the Government of the day was requested to send fifty young men to be trained as engineers and to prove themselves among the workers of England. But they had become weary of the hand-picking, so they decided to advertise and select. The next letter that came advised me to collect my passport and my wardrobe of winter clothes which consisted of a pair of rubber boots, a raincoat and a metal helmet. We all tried them on for laughs.

The crossing to England, in convoys of tankers and freighters, was extremely traumatic. They were torpedoed twice and lost their possessions, as well as suffering injuries. On arrival they were sent to an industrial town in northern England.

> In Manchester, England, we were placed on another train which took us to a quiet country town called Bolton. The Colonial Office told us that we were taken to Bolton because, of all the people in England, it was the people of Lancashire who seemed to be more capable of being sympathetic to people of colour, having employed several West Indian cricketers. So it would seem as though being able to play cricket had done more for West Indian people than anything else. The people of Bolton were notified of our arrival and our reasons for coming by way of the local newspaper. Some of them soon visited, offering their help.

The West Indians were housed in a spacious hostel – a "Colonial House" – where they were visited by locals and featured in the Bolton newspaper. However, conflict broke out between Barbadian and Jamaican students, and the two factions had to be accommodated separately. By day they studied at a technical college.

> In the morning it was drawing and studying blue prints and how to interpret them. In the afternoon, it was the workshop: learning to set up machinery and making parts from metal. Making bolts and nuts to fit. There were also English students learning at the same time and a good camaraderie was built up. After four months of study, we were placed into the factory as machinists.

They were not forgotten by those who had invited them to England, even if their own islands' governments seemed indifferent to their well-being.

> Never a word was heard from the Barbadian Government. As far as they were concerned we did not exist, but the Colonial Office one day sent one of their representatives and they had us assemble at the college. The official expressed his appreciation of us and told us that we were heroes and ambassadors for our country and we were brave for all that we had gone through and he wished us well. We were heartened by his words, we were greatly encouraged.[3]

The men remained in northwest England until the end of the war, working in industries in and around Manchester. "The West Indians, for the most part, worked at the Ford Motor Company, situated in Trafford Park. We made crank shafts for fighter planes, starting from a hunk of steel to the final crank with a tolerance of two thousands of an inch." And the government's choice of location seems to have been vindicated: "Throughout World War II the West Indians worked in Manchester with never such as a word of discord between them and the people of Manchester whether at work or at home or in places of entertainment."[4]

As soon as the war ended and the demand for combat aircraft ceased, the West Indian workers became redundant. They had the option of passage home or staying in Britain, though the Colonial Office made it clear that they would no longer be entitled to any official help.

> The Colonial Office was no longer responsible for us if we stayed. We would have to look for our own jobs and places of abode. The Colonial Office held that they had done quite enough for us: they had taught us a trade and sent us to the University of Manchester, where we had undergone twelve weeks of training as workshop foremen. So with this knowledge, we should be able to make quite a mark in our home islands.[5]

In fact, there was little prospect of suitable work at home, and the skills these men had acquired were therefore less useful than they had hoped. Nevertheless, they had been able to both make a satisfying contribution to the war effort and have a relatively pleasant stay in Britain.

Lumberjacks

Another scheme was to import foresters from British Honduras – where unemployment was at 30 per cent – to work for the Forestry Commission in Britain. Timber was of vital importance to the war effort. In peacetime Britain had been able to obtain it in large quantities from Scandinavia and the Baltic region. With this area now under enemy control, it became necessary to exploit sources at home more effectively. The demand for timber during the previous war had been so enormous that in 1919 the Forestry Commission had been set up to replace the losses and create a reserve for the future. This had proved a wise investment, and by the 1940s the first generation of trees had come to maturity.

Many thousands of acres in the remoter regions of Scotland and Wales were now covered with quick-growing coniferous forest, and it was there that the labour was needed. Foreign workers would replace British woodmen who had gone to the war, but several countries could provide the specialist skills necessary for efficient timber work, and the Hondurans were not the first to be called upon. Used to the mahogany trees of their own country and unused to the damp and cold of northern Europe, their services were requested only after contingents of Newfoundlanders, Irish, Australians and New Zealanders – as well as Italian prisoners of war – had already been put to work. The demand for men continued, and in May 1941 the governor of British Honduras received this communication from the Colonial Office in London:

> The Ministry of Supply [is] considering recruitment of a self-contained unit of about 500 skilled woodmen, as axemen and sawyers and would be glad to know whether suitable woodmen could be recruited from British Honduras. Unit would contain: Axemen, Sawyers, Blacksmiths, Cooks, Foremen and Specialists, etc. Only skilled workmen capable of felling a minimum of 2 and a half tons or 100 cubic feet of softwood a day would be accepted. If such men are available in British Honduras, Sir John Calder and the War Office would prefer that they come to [Britain] as civilian units on the same lines as the civilian forestry companies from Newfoundland. The War Office do not want them as military units. The cost per head as civilians is only half that of military units and there could be the question of equipment, etc., which would be difficult.

The issue of pay was clarified as follows: "The rates of pay are British rates. The wages proposed are arrived at by taking the basic time rate in the industry for adult home-labour of £3 per week (pay would be subject to British income-tax)." Though these were not high wages, the arrangement was to include free accommodation, clothing and provisions, together with a guarantee that the Ministry of Supply would pay their fares back to the Caribbean. The men were expected to sign contracts committing them to work for one year, or for the duration of the war – whichever was shorter (it was perfectly apparent in 1941 that the war would not end soon, and the term of engagement was later extended to three years). Though the initial request was for five hundred, almost nine hundred were to make the journey to Scotland over a period of slightly more than two years.

The British Hondurans were spiritual – if not actual – descendants of the loggers who had worked in that part of the Central American coast since the days of Spain's ascendancy, and they were as skilful as any lumberjack from Canada or Sweden. They were to be overseen by the Colonial Office but answerable to the Ministry of Supply. Like other labourers of this type, they would be housed in camps away from centres of population (their places of work were, in any case, extremely remote).

The scheme was plagued with difficulties from the beginning. As with the previous generation of West Indian volunteers in 1914–15, their passage to Europe was delayed, causing boredom and frustration. It was not until August, three months after the initial appeal, that shipping was arranged. For most of this time the men were unpaid, though they eventually received a token sum of 75 cents a day. When shipment of the contingent began, they were divided among several ships and sailed in a convoy, via Trinidad, Halifax and Iceland, across the North Atlantic at the height of the U-boat war, suffering a submarine attack on the way. They arrived in Britain without further mishap and were distributed to forestry camps, but delays in assembling and transporting the men meant that they had reached southern Scotland in late August, just as autumn was setting in.

The effect on West Indians who had known only tropical conditions was traumatic, and they began at once to fall prey to illness. Their clothing was unsuitable for the climate and, although warmer garments had been promised, it was only several months later – in the depths of winter – that they arrived. The men had no boots and many had to work in lightweight shoes. They had no gloves, and suffered particularly from having to handle frozen logs in bitter conditions. The trucks that brought them to and from the forests had no roofs, and the hastily constructed huts in which they slept were unheated except for a single stove in the middle (this was not evidence of official indifference to the men's welfare, as this arrangement was characteristic of the huts in which thousands of Allied servicemen lived throughout the war). Though a doctor based in Edinburgh was responsible for their health, there was no medical supervision on site. The Hondurans also found that the sections of timber to which they were assigned were frequently the most difficult to work, and were areas in which the other contingents – who, after all, had arrived first – had refused to work.

Initially there were few opportunities for recreation. The conditions proved so discouraging that absenteeism and drunkenness became common, and the men from the Caribbean quickly developed a reputation for obstinacy and inefficiency that was to dog them for the whole of their stay in Britain. As one of them later wrote,

> To Belizean mahogany cutters, the little – or rather minuscule – nature of the timber they had to fell in Scotland, compared to the huge size of a mahogany tree, made the timber seem no more than broom-sticks to them, and they devoured the forests in no time. Yet we were called "low producers" which is difficult to understand. We had new and very severe weather conditions to contend with, lack of official attention, illness and, of course, the level of poor food provided surely must have added to how good or bad we performed or were seen by an indifferent Ministry of Supply.[6]

Despite this unpromising experience, the ministry clearly still needed recruits from the Caribbean, for in the early months of 1942 it asked for another contingent. This time there were 341 men and they did not sail via Halifax, but were instead shipped to New Orleans for travel by train to New York. They sailed to the United States in an American vessel and on arrival were confined in a military camp outside New Orleans. There the US Army treated them the same way as African Americans in the segregated South. They were largely confined to the camp and, when briefly allowed to visit the city, reprimanded for showing friendliness to white women. They were given manual work, which some of them refused to do. As one later recalled, "We felt more like prisoners-of-war than volunteers travelling to the United Kingdom to do war work." They became surly and insubordinate as a result of the treatment they received, and this led white officialdom to see them as rebellious and uncooperative. They remained in New Orleans for almost a month, during which time they received a visit – and a lecture – from the British consul-general. His unquestioning acceptance of the camp authorities' version of events caused even further resentment.

This second contingent arrived in Britain to find weather conditions even worse than what their colleagues had met with the previous year. It was now the end of November, and they were dispersed to three camps in the north of Scotland, at Achnashellach and Kinlochewe on the west coast and at Golspie, north of Inverness on the more sheltered east coast. It would be difficult to imagine a greater contrast to the Caribbean than this bleak corner of the British Isles in the depth of winter. Like their predecessors, they found the living and working conditions a culture shock, but their camps were in fact less Spartan: some lessons had been learned by those responsible for their well-being.

The experience of the British Honduran foresters is often cited as a textbook case of mistreatment motivated by racial prejudice. It is implied that government officials, landowners and communities were openly reluctant to welcome or accept the men, who were largely ostracized. It was taken for granted that they would cause trouble, and the instances where they did were exaggerated. Local girls in particular were warned to have nothing to do with them. Far from home, living in sealed-off camps and with little incentive to work, most of the men became bitter. Closer examination, however, indicates that they were not as friendless among the local people as might be imagined, and that some of them were happy to remain in Scotland. Nevertheless, it cannot be denied that they suffered a good deal of neglect.

Because their welfare was the joint responsibility of two government departments whose duties were not clearly defined, each set of officials expected the other to take the necessary decisions – and spend the necessary funds – to solve any problems. Several of those who should have done so lacked sufficient interest or initiative, and the procedure for implementing improvements was as cumbersome as the civil service could make it. One of the officials involved – whose recollection suggests some sympathy for the men within the corridors of power – was later to write:

> On any matter of even the slightest importance we were expected to write to Mr Fitzgerald (at Bristol) who would then write to Sir S. Steel-Strang (at Edinburgh) who would then pass on the matter, with his compliments, either to General Carrington or to Mr Sangar, who in turn would then deal with Mr Robertson (the manager from British Honduras), Mr Keith has only just been able to break down this rather elaborate chain of communication. If as the Ministry now proposes, and we hope, they appoint a Welfare Officer, there ought to be no necessity for all this undue correspondence which so disturbs the hierarchy of the Ministry.[7]

Once the contingents began to become acclimatized, conditions improved. The necessary clothing and equipment became available, and spring and summer brought weather that made living and working more agreeable. The camps received occasional visits from musicians and ENSA performers, and there might also be evening classes to combat boredom. And not all the local communities shunned or ignored the Hondurans. The Scots are by tradition a hospitable people and, whatever reservations they may have had about exotic strangers in their midst, they proved increasingly kind. Many of the men were invited into the homes of local people, often for the weekend so they could enjoy the luxuries of baths and clean clothes, and they were able to mingle with other civilians in the pubs and dancehalls of the cities. Though they experienced some racial prejudice, this was balanced by a good deal of genuine kindness – as witnessed by the fact that some Hondurans married local girls and remained in Scotland after the war.

However, the overall picture was a negative one. The men had little faith in the government bodies that supervised their lives. Not only did they find conditions harsh, the weather also prevented them from earning the sums they had expected, for they were paid nothing for days on which no work could be done. A further blow was that their board and lodging, despite the promise that it would be free, turned out to be deducted from their earnings.

Weariness with the scheme on both sides – the foresters and the government – led to disbanding of the contingent and the return of most of its members to the Caribbean in the autumn and winter of 1943. The Ministry of Supply used the excuse that there was now sufficient timber and that no more cutting was necessary. As British citizens, however, the men were eligible to take any other jobs they could find in Britain. While many wished to return home as soon as possible, about a quarter of them, motivated by patriotism or the need to keep earning, opted to remain and stay in the war effort. An attempt was made to enrol some in the Royal Navy, but in the end they were found positions in industry and transport, with many taking jobs on the railways.

The men had come to Britain at the invitation of the government, yet the departments responsible had seriously neglected both their work and their welfare. Clement Attlee, Britain's deputy prime minister, looked into the situation: "The unit, having got a bad name at the beginning of its career, has been treated . . . with annoyance and suspicion, a point of view which was fully appreciated by [them]. . . . they had been given timber to cut which was situated in very difficult ground and which had been refused by other units." He added: "The attitude of the Ministry of Supply seems to be one of indifference. . . . Welfare organization, insofar as it does exist, is pitifully inadequate."[8]

It was assumed by people at all levels in British government and society that West Indians would not be able to live in the British climate, that they would be constantly ill and therefore unproductive (the experience of the First World War largely endorsed this view). Because of the slower pace of life in the Caribbean, it was also imagined that they would have difficulty keeping up with their work. A universal underlying principle of the Empire was that sexual relations or marriage between races was unacceptable; because men away from home were expected to be promiscuous, it was seen as imperative that women should avoid them. It was doubly unfortunate that this experiment placed the men in some of the remotest areas of Great Britain, and there can be no doubt that the unhelpfulness of the Ministry of Supply doomed the scheme from the beginning. A Colonial Office official wrote:

> If the British Honduran men are sent back . . . we shall have cries of colour discrimination that would perhaps not be easy to answer. It seems to me that the Ministry of Supply really want to send the men back because they have mismanaged the whole show and want to cover up before it's too late.[9]

It is worth noting that many West Indians volunteered for war work in Britain, more than forty thousand did so in the United States, and even more were involved in important work – building American bases – in their home islands.

Women

Those who sought uniformed service in Britain also encountered prejudice – or, at the very least, reluctance – on the part of the authorities. A case as notorious as that of the Honduran lumberjacks involved Caribbean women who wished to join the Auxiliary Territorial Service (ATS). Recruiting in the colonies for this female army unit was discouraged, not least by the stipulation that applicants had to pay their own way to Britain to take up their duties. Many organizations took the view that, while they themselves had no objection to black recruits, they feared that others would create difficulties. A government official, Dame Rachel Crowdy, expressed this attitude: "Is the Service including colour in its ranks? I am, I believe, genuinely without prejudice as to colour, race or religion, but I should not like to encourage these girls to come over only to find that they would not be taken on by any of the Women's Services."[10]

West Indian ATS women in London. (Imperial War Museum, D21361.)

There was also the familiar argument that those used to a very different life would be unable to adjust. The War Office noted:

> Whilst there is an urgent need for recruits for the ATS, the question arises whether women from the Colonies would not be better employed in conditions familiar to them locally rather than in strange conditions in the UK. Standards of comfort etc. must of necessity vary considerably in different parts of the world and it is questionable whether the formation of mixed companies would be a satisfactory solution . . . the wishes of the Army Council would be met more by the formation of local women's uniformed organizations in the Colonies rather than the enrolment and transport of such women to the UK.[11]

One difficulty was that ATS staff were needed for the British military mission in Washington, and the United States had racial tensions of its own. The US Army, which was sending many troops to Britain, was still segregated, and it was assumed that the presence of black members of the British forces would create awkwardness in dealings with its major ally.

Gradually, through persistence, the deployment of black women gained acceptance. A turning-point came at a London conference

Barbadian ATS women at Government House, 28 June 1943. (Photo by Mrs Margaret Walcott.)

in April 1943, when the Colonial Office won over the War Office and ensured equal rates of pay. Helpful in this issue was the case of a Bermudian, Miss L. Curtis, who had been accepted for training under the impression that she was white, and who had successfully battled for the authorities to honour their commitment – so successfully, in fact, that by the time a contingent of young women arrived in London in December 1943, there was no question of reluctance to accept them. They were sufficiently exotic to be the subject of an article in *Hulton's National Weekly* magazine. The photographs of pretty, high-spirited young women enjoying the strangeness of a new environment probably reflect their outlook very accurately. The article described them:

Why have they come to Britain, these thirty girls from the West Indies – to a climate they'd read about – and to a countryside devastated by a winter such as they've never seen? They haven't come because they were in need of a job; in fact, most of them had excellent jobs over there. They're all educated beyond the School Certificate Standard and some of them were school mistresses before they joined up; one was a dressmaker, one a dental assistant, another a radio operator; most of the others were stenographers in lawyers' offices, and department stores, and one was secretary to the Commanding Officer of the South Caribbean Area. Some of them have been to Britain before, and knew what to expect. And there are some white girls in this party. This, indeed, is a society without a colour bar, and the coloured girls come over not to be segregated but to join the ATS in a state of equality with its white members.[12]

Margaret Clairmonte was a Barbadian who served with the ATS. Like the others, she was bright and capable and held a good job at home. Her family had already participated in Britain's wars (her father was a veteran) and she was therefore receptive when invited to join. Stories of colour prejudice notwithstanding, active recruiting for this service was clearly being carried out in the Caribbean. She remembered:

I was working in the Colonial Secretary's office in Bridgetown, [and] the UK Government sent down some representatives to recruit young Caribbean women for service in the Auxiliary Territorial Service in Britain. I had no hesitation in volunteering. My only hiccup was that I was not yet 21 and had to have the permission of both parents. Well, my father, who himself had served in the First World War, gave his o.k. right away, but my mother, it seemed, had to telephone every possible contact in the whole island to get their views before agreeing! So I signed up. This was in May 1943 and it was not until September of that year that we got the final call.[13]

Another recruit, Cynthia Boyd, from Dominica, recalled the journey to England as more of a joyful reunion than an ordeal.

To my delight I found that among those travelling to the UK were friends and acquaintances and even a former schoolfriend. From Trinidad we travelled in convoy to the UK via New York where I met relatives. We had been transferred to the liner *Queen Elizabeth* but had no escort as she was too fast for a U-boat to attack.[14]

Once across the Atlantic and in London, Margaret Clairmonte found arrangements in place to provide both training and hospitality.

This was a very far cry indeed from the reception given to the Honduran woodmen.

> We met the Colonial Secretary, and visited the West India Committee. In those days before the Colonies became independent there were no High Commissions and the W.I. Committee acted on behalf of many trading companies. It was in the offices of the West India Committee that we deposited our luggage etc. and it was their address that we used for correspondence especially from our homes – they would redirect mail to our respective camps. We were always welcome there and whenever we visited London we would check in there to see whether there was any mail from home or to collect a few things from our suitcases.
>
> The West India Committee also played a sort of hospitality role. During the years whenever we had leave – usually 48 hours or 7 or 10 days – we would be interested in seeing different parts of the country. And here the West India Committee would assist. We would write to them to let them know when our leave was coming up and where we would like to spend it and they would offer home hospitality with some friendly British home in that area if possible. Many of us took advantage of this kindness for, although the hostels were run very efficiently, many of them were not much different from being in camp. Another organization, the British Empire Society, now the Royal Commonwealth Society, also offered to find us home hospitality for our holidays. We were also welcome at their headquarters in London and we were sometimes invited to their functions.[15]

Similar consideration was shown in assigning the young women to duties after the completion of six weeks' training. All were posted to the Royal Army Ordnance Corps depot at Bicester in Oxfordshire. "This training and posting en bloc, we found out later, was by arrangement between the Colonial Office and the War Office so that individuals would not have to fend for themselves alone in this strange place."[16]

Cynthia Boyd did her training in Surrey before posting to a unit of the British Army – a life she thoroughly enjoyed.

> I cannot recall the name of the [training] camp but it was the one at which the Queen (then Princess Elizabeth) had been trained when

she joined the ATS. Then on to Scotland for training in signals –
subsequently to be attached to the Royal Corps of Signals. Posted to
various camps in the UK, I wound up at the War Office where it was
so interesting to be handling messages for Sir Winston Churchill,
though these being in code we had no idea of the contents.[17]

Margaret Clairmonte, meanwhile, became a clerk, and spent a
busy but enjoyable period of service.

We were always busy at work as this was the beginning of 1944
and Britain and her allies were getting ready for D-Day, so we
worked from about 7.45 a.m. until around 6 p.m., and three
days a week up until 9.30 p.m. There was also a night shift
for which we could volunteer and this I did sometimes – it was
quieter and for six weeks there were no parades or queuing and
we went to work in a truck. We had a day off and occasionally
a 48 hour pass, but we were not permitted to travel more than
25 miles from the camp. So we frequented the university city of
Oxford and other small towns around and about.
    During 1944 several more groups of West Indians came over
to Britain to serve in the Forces so we found we had many more
friends and family to meet up with. After D-Day and [as] things
went well for the Allies we were allowed to travel around in
the UK so we took advantage of this and visited many parts of
England, Scotland and Northern Ireland to check out places we
had read about or had connections through friends.

She made progress in her work, and could have remained in
the ATS after the end of hostilities, but she chose to return to the
West Indies.

With two sets of specialized training behind me I now became
a Grade 1 Clerk and was made a corporal. After a while I think
I was beginning to become quite homesick and was not really
interested in further promotions – I even declined a posting to
the War Office in London . . . .

Before departure, however, she had one final duty – to represent
her branch of the service in the victory celebrations.

At a suitable time after the cessation of hostilities there was a
Victory Parade in London. Two of us from our unit – the Pay

Clerk, another corporal, and I – were chosen to represent the unit and be part of the London ATS contingent. In preparation for this event which was mainly a 5-mile march through London, we had to go to camp for two weeks' training. It was an exciting time and a special privilege, of course.[18]

Airmen

The service that involved the largest number of West Indians was the Royal Air Force, which deliberately recruited them through the overseas training scheme it set up in 1940. Three thousand men from the Caribbean enlisted in the RAF between 1940 and 1942. Four thousand more arrived in Britain as ground crew between June and November 1944, and a further fifteen hundred came in the spring of 1945. Eighty-one women from the region also served between 1939 and 1945.

This was a far cry from the response achieved in the First World War, when British policy was not to encourage participation from the West Indies. The view then was that local recruits might best serve Britain in other ways. Clearly that policy was no longer applicable in the Second World War, a war that had started in Europe but now engulfed the rest of the world, including the Caribbean. The sense of kinship with Britain had also improved, and at a time when the "mother country" needed help. A major recruitment campaign was mounted that attracted many West Indians to take up the call to serve, not only in the armed services, but also in the merchant navy and in factories.

The airmen recruited were initially assessed locally, based on their educational qualifications and aptitude. In the main, the successful candidates travelled to Britain for training as flight crew or ground staff. An advertisement had appeared in some West Indian newspapers in 1940:

Recruitment for the Royal Air Force
It is notified for general information that applications from suitable candidates for Air Crew training, particularly those who are suitable for training as pilots are invited by the Royal Air Force. The age limit for the entry of pilots has recently been raised, and candidates may now be accepted up to the age of 31.

Details of the necessary qualifications and application forms can be obtained from the Commissioner of Police.

The Air Ministry announces that it would also welcome applications from men up to 50 years of age, who are medically fit, who are a) radio mechanics – either amateur or professional – with a thorough knowledge of the theory and practice of modern Super Hetrodyne (a knowledge of Morse is not required) or b) wireless operators who can send and receive Morse at 20 words a minute.[19]

British Fleet Air Arm, Trinidad. (*National Geographic*, June 1942.)

Most of the men recruited by the RAF did not fly. They were trained as ground crew – those invaluable teams of mechanics and maintenance staff who kept the aircraft operational. The fact that they were seldom assigned to duty as aircrew, the more glamorous – though undoubtedly more dangerous – form of service, was not necessarily evidence of colour prejudice. There were two other possible explanations. The first was given by a Trinidadian, George Powe:

One of the reasons there were few West Indian aircrew was that they were selected on the basis of their educational qualifications. As far as I can remember, you had to have the equivalent of five O-levels before you could become an aircrew member. So that immediately cut out a lot of people particularly in those days in the West Indies. In Trinidad, for example, there were only two large secondary schools. Since a very small proportion of the population had secondary education . . . only a very small percentage of people became aircrew.[20]

Gerald Beard suspected that the government of his island, Jamaica, had made a deal with Britain that its people would not be exposed to unnecessary danger. This could be the second explanation:

There was some scepticism by the Jamaican Government. Mr Manley . . . was the one who was outspoken that we should not be sent to the Front. He thought it was more reasonable that the Englishmen went to the Front and we came behind, so I suppose Jamaica and the British Government came to that agreement.[21]

Enough, however, got airborne (between three and four hundred, in fact, of whom seventy received commissions) to make a substantial contribution. Moreover, they earned no fewer than 103 decorations; Barbados alone won five Distinguished Flying Crosses and a Distinguished Flying Medal. They included two Jamaicans; Flight Sergeant Tucker, a fighter pilot who made four "kills"; Sergeant Lincoln Lynch, who won not only the Distinguished Flying Medal but also the Air Gunners' Trophy for 1944; and Wing Commander Ulric Cross, a Mosquito navigator and Pathfinder (one of the elite airmen who lingered over targets to identify them for bomber forces) who won the Distinguished Service Order (DSO).

Of those who enlisted in the RAF, none became more famous in later life than Errol Walton Barrow, a brilliant young man who went on to serve as prime minister of Barbados both before and after independence. In 1940 he had planned to study theology at Codrington College but instead went to England to join the RAF. Barrow qualified for aircrew and became a navigator/observer. He undertook further training in Canada through the Commonwealth Air Training Plan, sharpening his skills in air gunnery, signals and bomb aiming. As part of this training he participated in a highly appropriate task for a West Indian airman – providing support for convoys and hunting U-boats. He subsequently won promotion to sergeant and flew in bombing raids over Europe, perhaps the most dangerous type of war service. He logged forty-five missions and was commissioned as a flying officer just as the war in Europe ended.

In wartime Grenada another young man dreamed of becoming an RAF pilot in spite of two daunting obstacles, neither of which involved his colour. The first was that, at six feet four, he was too tall to fit into a fighter's cockpit. The second was that his father, the forceful Caribbean politician T. Albert Marryshow, was implacably opposed to the notion that any son of his would serve in the armed forces. His son Julian won him around, however, and sat the necessary tests. He solved the first problem by unstrapping his parachute when in the cockpit.

Young Marryshow joined up in Trinidad, which he happened to be visiting.

> It has been a closely guarded secret that Trinidad was the first RAF Pilot training centre outside of the United Kingdom. I applied to join the Air Cadet Training Scheme. The first course had already been selected and had commenced training. I was among dozens of applicants for the second course, and after a rigorous series of medical tests and interviews, I was among the twelve selected.

Of these, "[e]ight were successful and were shipped to England on a tanker carrying high-octane aviation fuel". Only two of the eight were to survive the war. After further training in England, he achieved the dream of every air-struck schoolboy by becoming a Spitfire pilot.

Julian Marryshow never experienced any difficulty regarding race, though he commented:

> Those who had never seen coloured people before looked at us in wonderment, but once we started to talk to them, all was well. I remember that some people asked me where I had learned to speak English and I astounded them by joking that I had learned it on board ship while we were sailing to England!

Later he was posted to a squadron of Rhodesians.

> Through the eyes of a West Indian, white Rhodesians and white South Africans shared the same apartheid philosophy.

Yet I was welcomed by all and sundry, giving me the impression that I was granted the status of Honorary White. We all got on extremely well together, even to the extent of sharing gift parcels containing food items.

At the insistence of his Rhodesian commanding officer, Marryshow was commissioned while with that squadron. In early 1945 the job of his unit – he was by now flying the formidable Typhoon fighter-bomber – was "to give close support to the Canadian Army in breaching the Siegfried Line strongly fortified along Germany's western border". He described how:

We had a Liaison Officer on the ground with the advancing Canadians who would call us up (there were always a couple of aircraft flying above the Canadians) asking us to "liberate" the village of, say, Calcar or Asperden, or whatever. The pilot would then look it up on the map, the Liaison Officer would fire a red cartridge to confirm the village, and we would dive-bomb and "strafe" the village with cannon and machine-guns. Another two aircraft would then move into the cab rank. The Canadians would then go in and instantly deal with the surviving German defences.

It should be mentioned that the Typhoon was a well-armed aircraft. It had four 20mm cannons, eight rockets and at times two 1,000 lb bombs. Its top speed was about 400 mph, reaching 500 mph in a dive. Not bad for a single-seat fighter.

Once the Canadians were through the Siegfried Line we concentrated on destroying the German V1 and V2 rockets and the railways, tunnels and bridges used for getting them to their launching sites. I was shot down by ground fire on one of the sorties attacking a railway bridge near Utrecht (in the Netherlands). Fortunately I was able to climb to 2,000 feet before the aircraft lost power and went on fire. I reported to my leader that I was about to bale out, whipped the hood back, attempted to stand on the seat with flames lapping around the cockpit and put the aircraft in a dive. I could not get out because my radio jack was still in its socket so I had to climb back into the aircraft, close the hood to shut the flames out, remove my helmet, reopen the hood and jump out, narrowly missing being hit by the tail. I pulled my rip-cord and waited with bated breath for the silk canopy to deploy. After hours, which was in fact fractions of a second, the lovely sight of the unfolded parachute brought a song from my heart to my voice. Looking down, I could see my aircraft being cremated in a smoking fiery glow and I saw a thick wood below me and hoped I would not become entangled and hung-up in the upper branches, but I landed safely.

And here is one of those unbelievable stories! A Dutch farmer eventually took me to the nearest RAF airstrip. After being checked out I was told to wait while they organized the Commanding Officer's Auster aircraft to fly me back to my unit. After a wee while the Auster taxied up. I opened the passenger door to throw my rolled parachute in when I was frozen in time, my eyes and my mouth wide open, with the parachute poised in mid-air and the sound of "blankety blankety! What the bloody hell are you doing here?" I was staring into the face of a classmate of mine from the Grenada Boys' Secondary School, Jellicoe Esellmont Norbert Scoon! Everyone in our school had a nickname and his was Ces. We reminisced for the forty-minute flight. I was overjoyed . . .[22]

His schoolfriend, like other Grenadians following in his footsteps, had joined the Trinidad Air Training Scheme and had also graduated to join the RAF.

Soldiers

The Caribbean also provided ground troops. When the war began in 1939 the islands' volunteer forces were embodied and became a form of Home Guard, employed as coast-watchers and guarding government installations, other vulnerable points and prisoners of war. Because of the historical connection between the Caribbean and Canada, a number of men travelled north to enlist. These volunteers were collected together as contingents, but on arrival were scattered throughout the Canadian armed forces as necessity, or talent, dictated. Many went into the Royal Canadian Army Medical Corps as orderlies, ambulance drivers or stretcher-bearers. Others joined the artillery or went into armoured or signals units, and at least one ended up in the Canadian Grenadier Guards.

However, in October 1942 all local forces were taken under Imperial Command, the region becoming the Caribbean Area, with its headquarters in Jamaica (its commander was Brigadier Stokes-Roberts of the British Army). Under it were the North Caribbean Force (headquarters in Jamaica and comprising battalions from Jamaica, Bermuda, the Bahamas and the Leeward Islands) and the South Caribbean Force (headquarters in Trinidad, with battalions from Barbados, Trinidad and the Windward Islands).

Men in both forces who volunteered for active service overseas were formed into the First Caribbean Regiment; they trained in the United States before being deployed to the Mediterranean theatre of war. A Second Caribbean Regiment was formed, but hostilities ended as they were about to embark for overseas. One volunteer for service overseas has described the composition of this force, in which men from the islands with the most notorious rivalry were kept strictly apart by being enrolled in different companies.

On March 6th 1943 I enlisted in the Windward Islands Battalion at the Vigie Barracks. There I received my initial training inclusive of drills, obstacle courses and weapons practice.

In April 1944 I was amongst a contingent of 36 that journeyed to Trinidad. We waited in Trinidad for about two weeks for the arrival of troops from Barbados, British Guiana, Trinidad and the Leeward Islands. We then travelled to Jamaica on board the S.S. *Colombie* where we joined troops from there as well as from the Bahamas, British Honduras and Bermuda. We then proceeded to Newport News, Virginia, USA.

There we were constituted into the First Battalion of the Caribbean Regiment consisting of 1,200 troops. There were four companies:

A – Troops from Bermuda, Bahamas, British Honduras and Jamaica.
B – Troops from Trinidad.
C – Troops from Barbados.
D – Troops from the Windward Islands and British Guiana.

Additionally there were reinforcement and supply companies, which drew troops from all the territories.

In June on the King's birthday we celebrated with a parade. It was noted that not since the American War of Independence had there been so many British soldiers on American soil.[23]

The *Barbados Advocate* published pictures of this event and an article that stated:

The 1st Caribbean Regiment, consisting as it does of units from the South and North Caribbean Area is representative of all the islands of the West Indies and British Guiana, as well as Bermuda. Its formation in 1942 gave the men of these parts the long awaited opportunity to do their bit in an active theatre of war, and so maintain a long established tradition of fighting service.

Previous campaigns had found W.I. youth ready, willing and capable, and they gave sterling accounts of their worth in various parts of the world. This Caribbean Regiment is the first separate combatant contingent to be sent overseas in this war. It has its own supporting weapons including Bren guns, mortars and anti-tank guns, and is expected to take its place, as a full-fledged unit of the line, along with Allied infantry units.

Its ultimate destination is, like that of any other fighting unit, unknown, but on whatever field, it is determined to acquit itself as worthily as did its predecessors – the West India Regiment in the Cameroons in 1914–15, in German East Africa, or the BWIR battalions in the attack by the British on the Turkish positions in the Jordan Valley in September 1918.

Fighting in the common cause, alongside forces not only of Great Britain and the British Empire but also of America, is to have been admitted into the wide comradeship of arms, which will forge bonds that will be one of the greatest assets after the war. For when the war has been won will come the task of maintaining the peace – maintaining in the world the principles of truth and justice for which we are at present fighting.

But meanwhile the activities of the 1st Caribbean Regiment will be followed with the keenest interest by all within the West Indies. They take with them the fullest confidence of those left behind, and they hope to prove worthy of that confidence.[24]

In fact the war was to end before these high hopes could be realized, but in the meantime their training was intensive and realistic. Brigadier Stokes-Roberts, who visited them during this period, broadcast his impressions on radio for the benefit of those they had left behind. He described how, during one exercise,

The whole Battalion, including officers and their batmen, had to crawl more than 200 yards through trenches and shell-holes and a barbed-wire entanglement while an incessant hail of machine-gun bullets and light artillery shells was being poured over them not more than a foot above their heads and high explosive shells, represented by quite heavy charges of explosive, were detonated in close proximity to the crawling men. This exercise was carried out both by day and night, and during the latter period powerful searchlights lit up the area almost blinding the troops.

I am glad to say that the whole Battalion acquitted themselves well on both occasions and that there were no casualties. Generally speaking, our troops were in excellent health, but owing to cold at nights and in the early mornings there was a certain number of coughs and colds. All ranks were very well housed and the feeding was excellent, if anything too good, for I am afraid that when these men are on an active front they won't be getting the same luxuries.[25]

In June 1944 – the month in which the Allies invaded mainland Europe – the West Indian troops were shipped across the Atlantic. They were not, however, to be sent to the fighting in France; they went instead to southern Italy, which had been liberated the previous year, and for the rest of the war were given routine garrison duties far from the "sharp end". One of them, quoted earlier, summed up the rest of his military career:

Following training in Virginia we journeyed in June 1944 to Naples, Italy where in a camp, at the base of Mount Vesuvius we received further training. In December of that year we escorted 5,000 Germans to prisoner-of-war camps in Egypt, arriving at Port Said. We then journeyed to the desert near the town of Suez, where we undertook further training until the end of the war.

In December 1945 we left Egypt and the Caribbean Regiment was officially disbanded. I arrived back in St Lucia via Bermuda

and Jamaica in January 1946. In March I was transferred to St
Vincent and then back to St Lucia in August. The Battalion was
disbanded on July 4th 1947 and I re-entered civilian life.[26]

The Caribbean Regiment in Egypt, 1945. (Imperial War Museum, E31212.)

Ironically, in the Second World War West Indian soldiers served
in the same area – the Suez Canal and its surroundings – in which
their forebears had been stationed during the 1914–18 conflict.
They had, however, not been called upon to fight and had seen
even less action than the previous generation. There had been no
opportunity to win the commendations of senior officers as had
the BWIR thirty years earlier, and they made their biggest contribution by guarding prisoners, ironically the same task they had
performed in Jamaica as Defence Company volunteers.

The defeat of Germany, and then of Japan, brought an end to
the wartime coalition of great powers and colonial territories.
The Caribbean experience of wartime service had been a largely
negative one, just as it had been for the previous generation in the
Great War – a story of undervalued loyalty, unwanted assistance
and frustrated enthusiasm. The British authorities seemed unable
to grasp this, and even felt that the war had increased the loyalty
of overseas territories to the mother country. Harold Macmillan,
a future prime minister who was then under-secretary for the
colonies, said:

We must see to it that the comradeship and partnership which are growing up between us during the war continue into the days of peace, for they will be difficult and exacting days. And the whole concern – the Colonies and ourselves – must stand together, for security, for trade and for a common ideal and purpose of life. The pioneer days lie behind. The great days lie ahead.

With a similar lack of perspicacity he made light of the rejection that many black volunteers had felt in Britain.

The Colonial Office and the Government can do some things, but only on official lines. They can provide rest camps and welfare huts and clubs, and so on. But that's not the real thing. The real welcome can only be given by one man to another. Give him that, and send him back a convinced Ambassador of Empire. For, you know, we can be pretty stand-offish, and sometimes pretty rude without meaning to. Let him understand that we don't mean it, and what we really mean is friendship and comradeship.[27]

Though some individuals did carry home with them memories of welcome and kindness, the war had perhaps, more than anything else, hastened the desire of the Caribbean territories to leave the Empire altogether.

PART 3

The Sea War and the Role of Enemy Submarines in the Caribbean

CHAPTER 13
The War at Sea: The Setting

The importance of the region to the Allies' efforts in the War.

During the Second World War, the Allies in the war against the U-boats lost a total worldwide of 2,603 merchant ships and 175 warships. Of this total the Allies in the Caribbean lost exactly 400 merchant ships, with a further 56 damaged. Ninety-seven German and 6 Italian U-boats operated in the Caribbean from February 1942 until April 1945. Of these, only 17 U-boats were sunk while operating in these waters. This number represents only 2 per cent of the total 784 U-boat losses worldwide, and it means that Germany sunk 23.5 merchant ships for each U-boat lost in the Caribbean; to put it another way, each enemy U-boat operating in these waters sunk on average four ships. This probably made the Caribbean the most cost-effective campaign the Germans fought during the war.

On the afternoon of 11 September 1942, the German submarine U-514, under the command of Kapitänleutnant Hans-Jürgen Auffermann, was cruising at periscope depth just outside Barbados's Carlisle Bay. Reginald Gooding, a local school boy, witnessed what then occurred.

> That Saturday afternoon Dick Davies and I were in a dinghy some distance to the west of the anchorage of the yawl, *Pansy*, at that time the flagship of the Barbados Yacht Club fleet. I don't recall what we were doing out there, probably just going for a row out to the anti-torpedo nets which stretched across the bay from Needham's Point to Pelican Island, or going to take a closer

look at the S.S. *Cornwallis*, a frequent visitor to the island, which was unloading cargo to lighters from her anchorage in the bay. Certainly it wasn't an unusual place for us to be.

Located as we were, we had a grandstand view of the events that started with a bang at about 4.30 that afternoon. I remember vividly our shock at the first explosion. We knew almost immediately that it had occurred at the anti-torpedo net, for on looking out to sea we saw pieces of buoy and net blown high into the air. We were still assimilating this very unusual occurrence in our peaceful bay when a second explosion blew up another section of the net. Everything happened so fast and furiously for the next half-hour or so that I am unable to remember the exact sequence of events. The four-inch gun on Needham's Point started firing. The gun on the *Cornwallis* started firing. The net blew up in two more places. We had by then realized that the island was under attack, that it must be a submarine, and we were pulling like mad for the shore. We decided instead to go aboard the *Pansy* and that is where we were when the final torpedo found its way through the breached net and struck the *Cornwallis* about amidships.[1]

Despite Auffermann's firing six expensive torpedoes, *Cornwallis* was quickly beached, repaired and made seaworthy again. This sudden, noisy and unexpected occurrence caused great excitement in Barbados and is to this day the best remembered and most frequently talked about episode from the five years of the Second World War. But it was merely a trivial incident in the dramatic campaign being waged in the Caribbean between some five thousand officers and seamen of the German submarine fleet and many thousands of Allied sailors, airmen and soldiers.

SS *Cornwallis*, a 5,500-ton Canadian merchant ship, was badly damaged by U-boat 514, a Type IXC submarine commissioned in December 1941. After the engagement off Barbados, its twenty-eight-year-old commander, Hans-Jürgen Auffermann, continued his patrol by sailing south to the mouth of the Amazon River and the waters off French Guiana before returning to his base in France. During the patrol, which lasted ninety days, Auffermann sank five ships totalling 17,354 tons, in addition to the damaged

SS *Cornwallis*, temporarily repaired after being torpedoed in Barbados. Photo: Captain W.H.R. Armstrong. (Warren Alleyne, *Barbados at War, 1939–1945* [Barbados: Warren Alleyne, 1999].)

Cornwallis. On 8 July 1943, five days after leaving its base in Lorient, U-514 was caught on the surface in the Bay of Biscay surrounded by Spanish fishing boats. An aircraft from 224 Squadron, RAF Coastal Command, attacked and sank the submarine with depth charges; there were no survivors.

SS *Cornwallis* was repaired and taken back into service, but on 1 December 1944 it was torpedoed and sunk off the coast of Maine by U-1230, commanded by twenty-seven-year-old Hans Hilbig. In Barbados it is believed to this day that, after the war, the skipper of *Cornwallis* sought out and got to know the widow of Hans-Jürgen Auffermann.

In both world wars Great Britain was hugely dependent on ship-borne trade, a trade essential to keeping its population of some fifty million alive and its armed forces operating in the field. All its imports, whether from the Americas, Africa or the Far East, had to come across the North Atlantic. For the British, Canadians, Americans and Germans alike, the North Atlantic was a decisive battleground between the German U-boat fleet and the naval and air forces of the Allies. Nevertheless, operations in other oceans and seas had a significant influence on the course of the Battle of the Atlantic, and none had a greater influence than the campaign in the Caribbean.

Of all the imports to the United Kingdom in wartime, none was more important than oil. Britain had access to oil sources in the Far East and the Persian Gulf, but their output was consumed locally in those theatres of war. Thus oil for the United Kingdom and its armed forces came almost wholly from the Americas: the Dutch Antilles (Aruba and Curaçao), Venezuela and Texas. And in 1940 Trinidad had the largest oil refinery in the British Empire. The oil tanker was therefore of supreme importance – for the enemy to sink and for the Allies to protect.

The British Admiralty had learnt during the perilous month of April 1917, when the fledgling German submarine force sank 800,000 tons of shipping, that the most effective way to protect shipping was the convoy system – large numbers of assorted merchant ships assembled, escorted and protected by warships of the Royal Navy. This system, however, had two weaknesses: the whole convoy had to move at the speed of the slowest vessel – usually six knots – and its protection demanded great numbers of destroyers and other escort vessels.

The maritime situation for Britain in the summer of 1940 was very grave. By then the Royal Navy had only 171 destroyers worldwide, and of those almost half were out of action because of U-boat attacks, losses inflicted by mines laid in England's coastal waters, and losses or severe damage by the German air force – the Luftwaffe – during the evacuation of the British Army from Dunkirk. The result was a dire shortage of naval ships for convoy escort duties. The situation in the North Atlantic had turned dramatically against the British in June 1940, when France was defeated and overrun by the Germans. In consequence the whole of the European coastline, from the North Cape of Norway south to the Spanish frontier, was now in German hands, together with the great French naval ports on the English Channel and on France's Atlantic coast. By the autumn of 1940, the beginning of the crucial Battle of Britain between the RAF and the Luftwaffe, and with Germany anticipating an imminent invasion of England, Britain had lost an alarming number of ships.

Although the United States was neutral at this point, its government viewed with rising alarm the perilous situation that Britain faced and the growing threat of war with Japan. President Roosevelt, despite fierce opposition from a significant segment of the American people, resolved to strengthen the strategic position of the United States, initially in two ways. The US Navy handed over to Britain fifty destroyers; these escort vessels were refitted and became operational in October 1940, with forty-four in the Royal Navy and six in the Royal Canadian Navy. The US Navy also carried out a far-reaching review of the maritime defences of the nation, especially in the Caribbean region.

At that point in the war the Caribbean had bases in Jamaica and Trinidad (British) and Aruba, Curaçao and Bonaire (Dutch); these territories were friendly to the United States. The United States had already established its own bases in Florida (Key West), Guantanamo Bay (Cuba), Puerto Rico and the Panama Canal Zone. But in mid-1940 new dangers for the United States appeared in the region. Although Germany held no territory in the Caribbean, the islands of Martinique and Guadeloupe and the mainland territory of French Guiana were controlled by France, which was now collaborating with Nazi Germany – a situation that the German navy would undoubtedly exploit. Moreover, Brazil, Venezuela and Argentina were home to significant numbers of German citizens who were loyal to the Nazi regime and capable of carrying out hostile acts. In exchange, therefore, for the fifty destroyers from Roosevelt, Churchill authorized the United States to lease land and set up additional bases on six British-owned colonies: the Bahamas, Jamaica, Antigua, St Lucia, Trinidad and British Guiana.

In December 1941 the course of the war changed dramatically. The Japanese navy attacked the US naval and air force base at Pearl Harbor in the Hawaiian Islands, and Hitler, in support of Japan, his distant ally, declared war on the United States (as did Italy's Benito Mussolini). The United States was thus committed to a naval war in two oceans, the Atlantic in the east and the Pacific in the west.

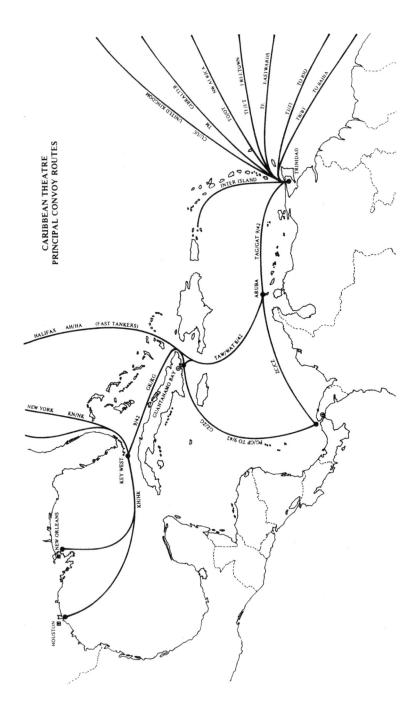

Main convoy routes in the Caribbean. (Gaylord Kelshall, *The U-Boat War in the Caribbean* [Shrewsbury, UK: Airlife, 1994].)

The United States and its principal allies, Britain and the Empire, were immediately joined by Cuba, and later by Mexico and Brazil. Venezuela and Colombia, though neutral, remained firmly under American influence. The massive work to construct six bases on the leased British land was put in hand at once, and large numbers of American servicemen moved in. They were armed to deal primarily with attacks by saboteurs, aircraft and surface vessels. At that stage the Americans rather discounted the submarine threat to the Caribbean, though the more experienced British did not.

Despite righteous anger and the demand for retribution against Japan that surged up among the American people after Pearl Harbor, it is hugely to the credit of the United States that it agreed with the Allies' strategy of defeating Germany first and Japan only thereafter. But, at the beginning of 1942, the naval defences along the east (Atlantic) coast of the United States were woefully unprepared for war. To defend three thousand miles of coastline and protect the vast number of ships sailing up and down those coastal waters, the US Navy had very few destroyers, only twenty smaller escort vessels and one hundred assorted aircraft. The commander-in-chief of the US Atlantic Fleet, Admiral Ernest King, determined from the first days of the war that his primary task was to safely escort ships carrying American men and material across the Atlantic, to the British Isles and later to the Mediterranean theatre of war. He gave a lower priority to dealing with naval threats in the South Atlantic and the Caribbean and so allocated fewer naval and air assets. Admiral King was much criticized for this policy, but events, as will be shown here, vindicated his judgement.

Nevertheless, the situation presented to Admiral Karl Dönitz, the commander of the German U-boat fleet, opportunities for spectacular successes against Allied shipping, and brought to the inhabitants of the West Indies dangers and trials such as they had not experienced for 150 years, and which until now have not been fittingly recognized.

CHAPTER 14
The War at Sea: The Unseen Foe

German U-boat successes with Italian co-operation.

Germany's strength as a naval power had traditionally been its submarines. Though it possessed a surface fleet in the First World War, this did not prove effective; the only major battle in which it took part – at Jutland in 1916 – was indecisive. Both sides claimed victory, but Germany's fleet remained bottled up in port until the end of hostilities, and took no further part in the war. However, German submarines – U-boats – were free to roam the Atlantic and the North Sea, and they proved a potent weapon. Germany, itself subject to a blockade throughout the war, had attempted to starve the British Isles into surrender by cutting off their supplies of food and raw materials. The U-boats proved effective, their most notorious action being the sinking in 1915 of the passenger ship *Lusitania*, but Germany's policy of "unrestricted submarine warfare" – attacking any ship, regardless of its status – led the United States to declare war in 1917. In the course of the conflict, German submarines sank eleven million tons of Allied shipping, but international vilification was a heavy price to pay.

Derived from the German *Unterseeboot*, meaning "under-sea boat", the term U-boat is used to denote all German navy submarines, including submarines that served with the Austro-Hungarian navy up to 1918. Deployed against commerce and skilfully handled, German submarines came close to achieving decisive results in 1917, but the number of boats at sea (never more than sixty-one) was insufficient to completely paralyse Allied maritime communications. Wartime losses were very high, with 192 boats sunk or interned before the armistice in 1918 and more than fifty-four hundred crew killed. When a serious mutiny erupted in the German fleet in October 1918, the officers and men of the U-boat arm did not join in.

The postwar settlement made at Versailles by the victorious Allies forbade the German navy to have any U-boats. Nevertheless, the new German republic continued to develop submarine technology and to train crews in secret. Other countries – the Soviet Union, Spain and Turkey – made use of German technology and expertise in creating their own submarine fleets. While building boats for them, Germany was able to lay the groundwork for its own U-boat arm and to give its sailors valuable experience during sea trials. The cloak of secrecy was removed in 1935, when the Anglo-German Naval Agreement was signed. This arrangement, part of the British government's appeasement of Hitler, gave the German navy the right to have a submarine force, providing it did not exceed 35 per cent of the size of Britain's. The following year the Spanish Civil War began and German U-boats were sent to support General Franco, the fascist rebel leader, thus providing intensive training for German submariners that went on until war broke out in September 1939.

Grand Admiral Karl Dönitz (1891–1980) was commissioned into the German navy in 1910 and was a submariner during the First World War. From September 1935 he commanded the U-boat arm of Hitler's navy; promoted to rear admiral in 1939, he led the U-boats with conspicuous success during the early years of the Second World War. His crews were superbly trained and their morale was enhanced by Dönitz's personal commitment to his commanders, who responded with panache and daring. In early 1943 he was promoted to grand admiral and became commander-in-chief of the German navy. His deployment of submarines after their Atlantic defeat in 1943 was largely defensive, pending development of new weapons to counter the Allied anti-submarine groups.

In 1945 Dönitz organized the evacuation of thousands of troops and civilians away from the Red Army's advance on the eastern Baltic, perhaps the most successful German surface operation of the war. At the end of April 1945 he was named Hitler's successor as head of state, and he negotiated the surrender of the German forces in the west. In November he was arraigned before the International Military Tribunal at Nüremberg on three counts: plotting to wage aggressive war, waging aggressive war and war crimes. Despite submissions in his defence by senior British and American naval officers that Dönitz had fought a "clean war", he was found guilty on the two latter charges and sentenced to ten years in prison, the lightest sentence awarded to any of those found guilty by that court.

In 1939 Dönitz had fifty-six U-boats, of which only nineteen were ocean-going. Moreover, in Hitler's eyes the navy (Kriegsmarine) ranked third in importance, below the army and the Luftwaffe; the head of the Kriegsmarine, Admiral Erich Raeder, had far less influence than the senior officers of the other services. But the officers and men of the submarine fleet, all volunteers, had been put through arduous and very thorough exercises in the Baltic, and their boats were well designed and built. In the first weeks of the war they had two major successes: on 17 September the aircraft carrier HMS *Courageous* was sunk, and on 14 October Lieutenant Commander Günter Prien, in a fine feat of navigation and daring, steered his U-47 through block ships, booms and hazardous currents into the naval anchorage of

Grand Admiral Karl Dönitz. (Imperial War Museum, A 14899.)

Scapa Flow. There he sank HMS *Royal Oak* with the loss of over eight hundred lives. The honour of the German navy had been sullied, however, on the very first day of the war, when a U-boat sank without warning an unarmed liner, *Athenia*, which was carrying many women and children across the Atlantic to the safety of the New World. Prien's success was greeted throughout Germany with jubilation, and so aroused Hitler's enthusiasm that he agreed to the immediate building of three hundred U-boats, aiming at a final fleet strength of nine hundred.

To cripple Britain's trade and bring it to its knees, the Germans knew they had to sink Allied ships at a faster rate than Britain, and especially the United States, could build them. By the end of 1939, 114 merchant ships had been sunk. In the following year escort craft became even scarcer as they were withdrawn from the Atlantic to defend the British Isles against the expected German invasion. U-boat crews were later to remember 1940 as "the happy time"; despite the small number of boats and major technical defects in their torpedoes (which scientists took two years to rectify fully), they were able to sink 3.4 million tons of shipping and, from their base in the Baltic, to patrol as far west as the coast of Newfoundland.

With the fall of France in June 1940, the Kriegsmarine swiftly took over five naval bases on the Atlantic coast. At Brest, Lorient, La Pallice, St Nazaire and Bordeaux the construction of large bombproof shelters was commenced. Dönitz transferred his (extraordinarily small) U-boat control centre from north-west Germany to Paris and later to a château at Kerneval, near Lorient, and his U-boats soon began operating from these French ports. Mussolini, who had meanwhile brought Italy into the war, offered Hitler the cooperation of the Italian submarine fleet in the vital Battle of the Atlantic. Hitler's advisers, aware of the deplorable reputation of their ally's navy, were reluctant to accept the offer, but Hitler overruled them on political grounds, and in late 1940 a force of thirty-two Italian submarines was based at Bordeaux under the command of Admiral Angelo Perona.

Notwithstanding the much more favourable strategic situation which the second half of 1940 and 1941 presented to

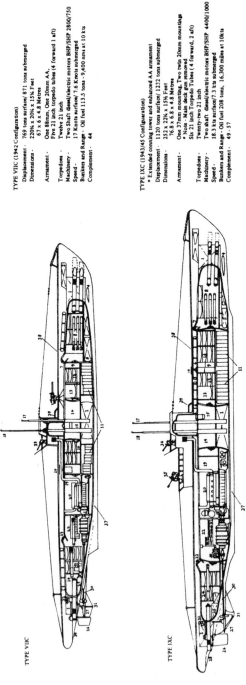

TYPE VIIC

TYPE IXC

TYPE VIIC (1942 Configuration)

Displacement -	769 tons surface/ 871 tons submerged
Dimensions -	220¼ x 20¼ x 15¾ Feet
	67 x 6 x 4.8 Metres
Armament -	One 88mm, One 20mm AA,
	Five 21 inch torpedo tubes (4 forward 1 aft)
Torpedoes -	Twelve 21 inch
Machinery -	Two Shaft diesel/electric motors BHP/SHP 2800/750
Speed -	17 Knots surface/ 7.6 Knots submerged
Bunkers and Range -	Oil fuel 113.5 tons - 9,400 nms at 10 kts
Complement -	44

TYPE IXC (1943/45 Configuration)

* Extended conning tower and enhanced AA armament

Displacement -	1120 tons surface/ 1232 tons submerged
Dimensions -	252 x 22¼ x 15¾ Feet
	76.8 x 6.8 x 4.8 Metres
Armament -	One 37mm mounting, Two twin 20mm mountings
	Six 21 inch Torpedo Tubes (4 forward, 2 aft)
	* Note - Main deck gun removed
Torpedoes -	Twenty-two 21 inch
Machinery -	Two shaft diesel/electric motors BHP/SHP 4400/1000
Speed -	18.3 kts surface/7.3 kts submerged
Bunkers and Range - Oil fuel 208 tons, 16,300 miles at 10kts	
Complement -	49 - 57

KEY

(1)	Main Ballast Tank	(9)	Galley	(18)	Attack Periscope
(2)	Stabilising Tank	(10)	Escape Hatch	(19)	Diesel air intakes
(3)	Bow Torpedo Tubes	(11)	Batteries	(20)	Main Diesel Engines
(4)	Fore Hydrophone	(12)	Officers Wardroom	(21)	Main Electric Motors
(5)	Forward Trim Tanks	(13)	Captains cabin	(22)	Control Panel
(6)	Spare Torpedo Containers	(14)	Control Room	(23)	Aft Torpedo Loading Hatch
(7)	Forward Torpedo Loading Hatch	(15)	Control Room Hatch	(24)	Aft Torpedo Room
(8)	Forward Torpedo Room and	(16)	Petty Officers Mess		Engineer Ratings Mess
	Torpedo Ratings Mess	(17)	Air and Sea Search Periscope	(25)	Spare Torpedo stowage
	Spare Torpedoes				Aft Trim Tank

(26)	Twin Rudders	(35)	37mm Mounting
(27)	Aft Hydrophone	(36)	Twin 20mm Mountings
(28)	Aft Torpedo Tubes	(37)	Pressure Hull
(29)	Aft Torpedo Tube	(38)	Deck Casing
(30)	Propeller Shafts	(39)	Compass Housing
(31)	Propeller and Rudder guards		
(32)	Steering gear		
(33)	Single 20 mm cannon		
(34)	88mm Main Deck Gun		

Cross-section of a U-boat. (Gaylord Kelshall, *The U-Boat War in the Caribbean* [Shrewsbury, UK: Airlife, 1994].)

Admiral Dönitz, the growing experience of the British sailors and airmen protecting the transatlantic convoys, as well as the help being provided by the (still neutral) US Navy and port authorities, was making the North Atlantic increasingly hazardous for enemy submarines – and ships. In May 1941 the Royal Navy cornered and sunk, with the loss of more than two thousand lives, the great German battleship *Bismarck*, which had been hailed as the most powerful ship in the world. The Germans needed therefore to extend their U-boat operations to more distant waters: the coasts of the United States and Canada and the Caribbean Sea were to become their fresh hunting grounds.

The Type IX U-boats were designed to operate far from European bases. Their fuel range allowed them to remain on station in the Caribbean for three weeks, plus outward and return journeys of two weeks each. This range could be extended by refuelling at sea from friendly merchant ships or specially built tanker U-boats. Their diesel engines allowed them to travel on the surface at eighteen knots; submerged, their electric engines gave them a speed of seven knots – slightly faster than the speed of the average convoy. Their armament consisted of twenty-two twenty-one-inch torpedoes, each with a six-hundred-pound warhead. These were fired from six tubes, four in the bow and two in the stern. On deck each boat had a four-inch gun, which was much used in surface engagements, and for protection against air attack, a set of deadly *flak* machine-guns. Very important for its protection against air attack was the boat's ability to "crash-dive" in thirty-five seconds, submerging to safety before the approaching aircraft could effectively attack. Built of the famous Krupp steel, these submarines could withstand the water pressure at six hundred feet, and some were to survive at greater depths. Moreover, they were difficult to damage fatally. To "kill" a submerged submarine, a depth charge had to detonate within some thirty feet of the hull, and air-dropped bombs within six feet. (In July 1944 one U-boat in the English Channel was attacked for thirty hours with more than a hundred depth charges and it survived.)

Living conditions inside a U-boat. (Clay Blair, *Hitler's U-Boat War: The Hunters, 1939–1942* [London: Weidenfeld and Nicholson, 1997].)

A U-boat was manned by a Kapitänleutnant, Korvettenkapitan or Oberleutnant zur See in rank, two watch-keeping officers, seven petty officers and thirty-nine ratings. Some of the officers had served before the war in German liners and merchant ships; a few already knew the Caribbean islands and waters. The oldest skipper was thirty-four, and the average age of the ratings was in the early twenties, though this fell to nineteen towards the end of the war. All were volunteers and, despite the cramped conditions, poor sanitation, dirt, foul air, fitful sleep, monotonous food and constant danger, their morale and self-esteem were remarkable. This was in great measure because of the character of their "chief" – Admiral Karl Dönitz was an experienced and trusted submariner, clearly dedicated to the efficiency and well-being of his officers and men. Moreover the successes of the U-boat arm were given maximum publicity at home, and Hitler awarded to every U-boat captain the Ritterkreuz (the Knight's Cross of the Iron Cross) on confirmation that he had sunk a hundred thousand tons of enemy shipping. The men of Germany's U-boat fleet were public idols, and the loss of any of their "aces" – the most successful commanders – was mourned by the whole nation.

Once at sea after detailed briefings from Dönitz's staff, individual U-boats were controlled by radio from the U-boat control centre, to which each boat regularly sent short, encoded situation reports and sightings of enemy shipping. Dönitz was greatly helped by his listening service (B-Dienst), which continuously monitored the wireless "chatter" of Allied ships. It was claimed that 80 per cent of this radio traffic was decoded and read, thus enabling Dönitz to deploy his submarines in the path of convoys and to group U-boats into the "wolf-packs" that attacked the North Atlantic convoys with such deadly effect.

The Allies also had listening services, manned by talented men and women who, by breaking the codes used by the Enigma machines of the different branches of the German armed forces, were able to predict with growing accuracy the enemy's plans and movements. This advantage was enormously magnified when an Enigma machine and its related codes and documents were secretly retrieved from a sinking U-boat in a courageous sortie. All this was a major factor in helping the Allies win the crucial Battle of the Atlantic.

Soon after the United States entered the war, Dönitz planned to send twenty-five U-boats on an initial foray (Operation *Paukenschlag*, or "Drumbeat") to the coasts of Canada and the north-eastern states of America, but Hitler, obsessed by fear of an Allied attack on Norway, reduced the number to fifteen. On the night of 14 January 1942, the first wave of three boats (U-123, commanded by Reinhard Hardegen; U-125, by Ulrich Folkers; and U-66, by Richard Zapp) struck at the coastal traffic off Norfolk, Virginia, and Canada. In ten days they sank ten ships, including four tankers, causing consternation and alarm. The Germans were astounded by the density of the shipping, all clearly visible against the background of an illuminated coastline, and the lack of defences. Indeed, Hardegen surfaced his U-123 off Manhattan to let his crew glimpse what they termed "the golden west". Later in

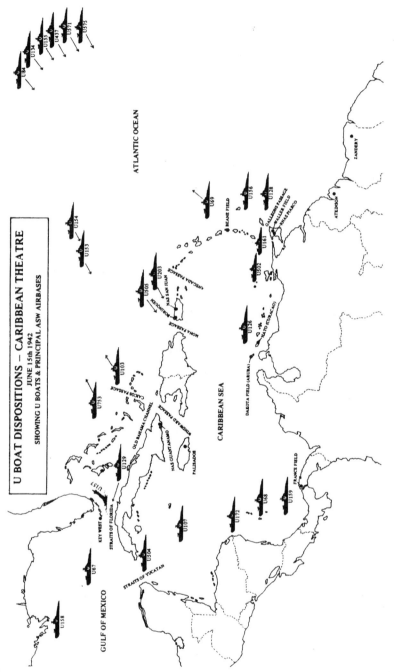

U-boats in the Caribbean Sea, June 1942. (Gaylord Kelshall, *The U-Boat War in the Caribbean* [Shrewsbury, UK: Airlife, 1994].)

January, twelve more boats were sent to operate off Nova Scotia and Newfoundland. Despite fearful weather, gales and ice, they accounted for twenty-two ships. During this, the first phase of *Paukenschlag*, these fifteen U-boats sank forty-one ships totalling a quarter of a million tons, including thirteen tankers. One U-boat was slightly damaged; none was lost.

At the same time Dönitz was planning an operation (*Neuland*) to prevent the flow of oil and bauxite from South America and the Caribbean. He dispatched five U-boats to patrol off the coast of Venezuela and six Italian submarines farther north, off the Windward Islands. The crews were ordered to concentrate on two vital but vulnerable targets. One was the pair of Dutch islands, Curaçao and Aruba, where half a million barrels of petroleum were produced every day. The other was Trinidad, which not only had its own supplies of oil but held even greater importance as a convoy assembly area and shipment point for the huge quantities of bauxite needed by the war effort. This commodity was brought downriver from the interior of British Guiana in shallow-draught vessels, ferried to Trinidad by a shuttle service of small craft, and transshipped at Port of Spain for the voyage north on American freighters.

The German U-boats attacked on 16 February 1942, under a new moon. The impact of their arrival was immediate and devastating. In Trinidad's Gulf of Paria six tankers were sent to the bottom in quick succession. That same night, U-161 entered the harbour at Castries in St Lucia on the surface (it was too shallow to dive) and torpedoed two ships at the quayside, sailing out again with no retaliation.

Operational conditions in the Caribbean were far better than off the American coast, and the U-boats were able to sink from six to ten ships each, with particularly good results off Trinidad, in the Strait of Yucatán and in the Gulf of Mexico. As shipping in the Gulf of Mexico was neither protected nor controlled, and in fact behaved as if in peacetime, it seemed the enemy had not yet reckoned with the appearance of U-boats in these waters.[1] By the time the U-boats left the Caribbean for France in March, they had sunk twelve tankers and damaged five others. In addition the

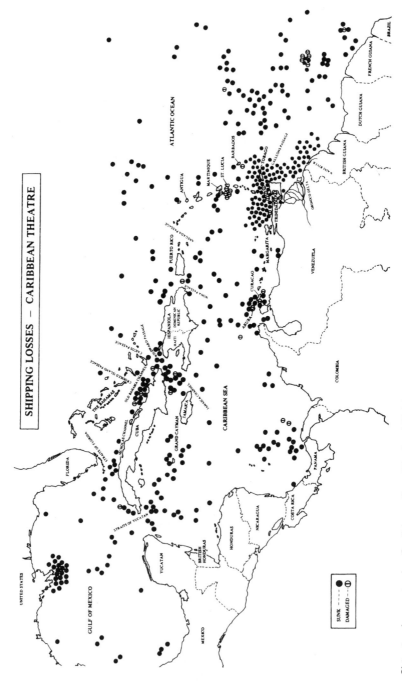

Shipping losses in the Caribbean Sea. (Gaylord Kelshall, *The U-Boat War in the Caribbean* [Shrewsbury, UK: Airlife, 1994].)

Italian vessels had sunk twenty ships, including nine tankers – the most successful coordinated blow struck by Italy's submarine fleet during the Second World War.

Delighted with the success of Operation *Neuland*, Hitler promoted Dönitz to the rank of four-star admiral. Dönitz, however, realized that the Allied reaction would be resolute, with Caribbean defences strengthened, convoy practices improved and air cover increased, and that shipbuilding in the United Kingdom, Canada and the United States would more than equal the losses. Moreover, these submarine patrols into seas so far from Europe, lasting more than sixty days and followed by lengthy refitting and recuperation, were less economic than operations nearer home. And, it must be noted in vindication of Admiral King's policy, while the enemy were enjoying a memorable "happy time" in southern waters, the navies of Britain, Canada and the United States had succeeded in sending nineteen convoys, totalling 450 ships, unopposed across the North Atlantic to Iceland and the British Isles.

After a lull during April 1942 caused by the need to refit and by abnormally severe ice in the Baltic, U-boats returned to the Caribbean. As the German Naval Historian has stated,

> All the operations were made possible by the arrival of the first U-tankers – U-459, U-460 and U-116. The availability for refuelling the operational U-boats in the Western Atlantic was of great benefit to the campaign, for our medium boats could not otherwise have been maintained in the Caribbean. Boats on outward passage were refuelled from these tankers so that they could start operations with a full load of torpedoes and fuel.
>
> Our primary objective was to exploit the unique opportunities in the Caribbean where we were able to maintain ten to twelve U-boats. With the six boats that were sent south from the American coast in the latter half of May, the Caribbean now became our main theatre of operations. The larger boats which came after were assigned to remote areas. Proceeding slowly through the waters traversed by their predecessors, they too interrupted their passage to attack shipping wherever encountered.

However, their quarry was learning to protect itself. In these waters the Allies' control of shipping and anti-submarine measures developed step by step towards proficiency, as had occurred off the American coast.[2]

Apart from the vulnerability of merchant vessels and their cargoes, which were targets too tempting to ignore, the German navy deliberately sought to operate across as extensive an area as possible so that Allied defences would be stretched widely and thinly. The sketchy nature of many defences meant that the submarines scarcely noticed them, and U-boat crews would leave the West Indies only when they ran out of fuel or ammunition.

During that summer U-564, commanded by Reinhard Suhren, entered West Indian waters in search of prey. An account of the mission based on Suhren's memoirs describes the sea war from the German viewpoint; it shows that even in the "golden west" the submarines did not always have things their own way. The crews faced nagging tension punctuated by outright terror.

> The startled cry that the entire crew dreaded to hear burst from the bridge: "*Flieger!*" A large enemy aircraft was closing rapidly from out of the sun, flattening out only twenty metres above the waves and heading rapidly into a low-level attack. Throwing the boat into its practised crash-dive routine, Gabler took her down as fast as possible, U-564 reaching such an acute angle that loose fixtures of all descriptions tumbled from their place and clattered noisily toward the bow. With mere metres of water over her bridge, three well-placed bombs bracketed the U-boat, severely shaking the hull and causing fresh chaos aboard. A thin jet of flame shot from the closed hatch to number five torpedo tube, prompting considerable alarm amongst the men as they manned the electric motors and diesel engines. However, there was no water leakage and the engineers could only assume that, though the tube may have been damaged by the bomb blasts, it remained watertight. Machine-gun fire peppered the water above U-564, although more to vent the Allied gunners' frustration than with any real hope of hitting the target. Men were nearly thrown from their feet, and U-564 staggered under the impact. Lights shifted and broken glass tinkled to the decking, unheard amidst the cacophony of disturbed water that pummelled the pressure hull. Suhren held his men under firm control, his quiet authority and unshakeable calm keeping in check any distress felt by his crew.

An atmosphere of professional calm descended over the crew, and the required bravado at another narrow shave with death passed among the men still lying where they had tumbled within the U-boat's bow compartment. In the control room, Gabler began to bring U-564 to trim and reported the depth as 60 metres. But, within seconds, both he and Suhren realized that something had indeed gone terribly wrong. Alongside the normal noises generated by the boat were strong echoing creaks and groans that shuddered through U-564's sturdy frames. To an experienced U-boat man, the distinctive noises could mean only one thing: they were plummeting downwards into the immense water pressure of extreme depth. The fear of slipping silently into the abyss until the pressure hull imploded suddenly gripped the entire crew, and Suhren ordered the forward tanks blown clear of ballast with compressed air. The boat's descent must be stopped, and her bow forced to rise if they were ever to regain the surface.

As compressed air hissed through pipes and into the ballast tanks, the freefall gradually tapered off and the bow perceptibly began to rise towards the horizontal. U-564's descent had been arrested at a depth of 200 metres, every frame screaming with the strain, but no visible leaks were found. An absolute hush descended over the entire boat as Gabler gingerly eased them away from the sea-bed thousands of metres below. U-564 gently ascended to a safer depth, and before long the engineering crew set about repairing the many systems that had taken damage, thanking their good fortune at sailing aboard a boat built in Hamburg.[3]

CHAPTER 15
The War at Sea: The Victors

The Allies mount counter-submarine measures.

The British and Americans steadily, albeit belatedly, improved their anti-submarine defences and techniques. Royal Navy air stations, HMS *Buzzard* and HMS *Benbow,* had been established in Jamaica and Trinidad, and the Swordfish aircraft of 835 Squadron were able to provide limited protection for shipping during the difficult first months of Operation *Neuland.* Though these aircraft were antiquated and had limited operational range, they could carry torpedoes or bombs, and their presence was somewhat reassuring. After settling into luxurious quarters, one flier recalled:

> The Squadron got down to anti-submarine patrols, armed with 250 lb bombs. It was reported that some twenty U-boats had been sent to the eastern coast of the USA and the Caribbean and were sinking large numbers of Allied ships of all nationalities, particularly tankers, which were sailing unescorted, due to the regrettable reluctance of the US Navy to introduce a convoy system.[1]

The convoy system was improved and ships sailed in groups on the familiar run to Halifax or New York to link up with the transatlantic supply route. However, U-boat crews continued to see the Caribbean and the South American coast as an opportunity to wreak havoc with relative impunity. As the German official history recorded, with reference to the first half of 1943:

> From January to May there were only five to ten U-boats in the coastal areas of the Central Atlantic, including the Caribbean –

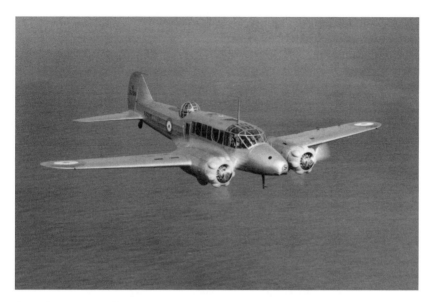

Avro Anson aircraft. Many West Indians were either trained on or flew this aeroplane. (Charles Brown Collection, Royal Air Force Museum.)

just enough to maintain pressure on the enemy. Convoys in the Caribbean and on the Brazilian and African coasts were not only less strongly escorted, but the escort vessels themselves were regarded by our men as being "harmless" in comparison with those in the North Atlantic. Whether this inferiority was due to lack of training or experience or to poor equipment we did not know, but to us it was a recognised fact, and at that time a single U-boat had a better chance of firing torpedoes at a convoy sighted in these areas than had a whole group of boats against a US–UK convoy.[2]

However, the escorts were doing their best. A member of the Royal Navy recalled the beginnings of this new phase:

We joined up with HMS *Brilliant* to form Escort Group B4. Our job was to start a convoy system from the Indies to the US, to link up with the Atlantic convoys. Ships had been sailing from South America unescorted until the U-boats found their way down into the old Spanish Main and made their presence felt. We were to work closely with the USN, to come not only under American command, but also USN victualling too. Going from the old traditional destroyerman's breakfast (a cup of tea, a fag and a good cough) to a Yankee three course breakfast was, we felt, going to make us all sadly overweight.

Our first convoy out of Port of Spain consisted of five ships, two of them leaving us on the first afternoon to go to Venezuela. The rest, a British freighter, an American tanker and a Belgian sailed on northward, escorted by *Churchill* and a Dutch corvette, *Jan van Brakel.*[3]

Another northbound expedition was better protected, as one British sailor remembered:

When we left Kingston, we teamed up with two other ships and a naval motor launch for the short journey to Cuba. Here we anchored in Guantanamo Bay for two days whilst a convoy was assembled for New York. We were escorted by two smart American destroyers and overhead we had the added vigilance of two blimps, small airships sent up for submarine spotting.[4]

Not all convoys went north. Some, headed for the garrisons in the Mediterranean, struck directly across the Atlantic. An account of one of these – and it describes an experience fairly typical of those undergone by West Indian merchant seamen – gives an impression of what life on these nerve-racking voyages was like: the large number of escort vessels, the partial protection of aircraft and, almost incidentally, the appearance of the German predators.

On the afternoon of Sunday 27th December 1942, B5 Escort Group arrived at Port of Spain, Trinidad. We were there for only a few hours and were to sail at 1.30 the next morning with a highly important convoy for Gibraltar – en route for Malta, which island was at this time under siege. There were nine tankers only in this convoy, six carrying Admiralty fuel oil and the other three high grade aviation spirit.

Shore leave was piped and those off duty were able to go ashore until 11 p.m. – their last fling before the eighteen-day trip to come, across the South Atlantic.

This convoy was designated "T.M.1" (Trinidad–Malta No. 1) and, according to plan, the nine great ships and eight escorts slipped out of the harbour at the appointed time, and were soon lost in the black of night. All was quiet as we made our way through the darkness – only broken periodically by the roar of engines as the Catalina Flying Boat that had been detailed to give us air-cover came zooming overhead every half-hour or so. Two or three hours later when we were well out to sea we were unexpectedly provided with what appeared to be a glorious firework display some twenty miles astern, with flashes, sparks and streaks of light shooting backwards and forwards between sea and sky. Our Yankee friend had spotted a U-boat and was giving him all he had! Things eventually settled down to normal and about thirty minutes later the Catalina was overhead again. He came right over our ship, HMS *Pimpernel*, and as he did so, our Captain picked up the R/T transmitter and said "Did you get him, pilot?" and in a slow Yankee drawl the answer came back through the bridge loud-speaker: "I guess I don't know – but I sure shook the hell out of him!"

That was early morning, 28th December, and a few days passed without incident – going on watch, coming off watch, eating and sleeping, lookouts constantly scanning sea and sky, and waiting for something to happen. Things did start to happen on 3rd January; a U-boat was sighted and an attack took place resulting in the sinking of one tanker. HMS *Saxifrage* rescued survivors but was only able to account for 14 out of 54.

A signal from the Admiralty warned us of a U-boat pack in our path, and our course was altered in an effort to avoid them, but they caught up with us on 8th January. This was a particularly heavy attack by night, and it was estimated that six or seven of the enemy were involved. Five ships were sunk in this attack, leaving three. *Saxifrage* rescued a further 60 men and the destroyer *Havelock* picked up 230.

We had no air-support now as the Catalina's fuel-supply would allow for seven hours before having to return, and calls for assistance had already been sent out to the authorities ashore.

On 9th January a cheeky U-boat commander surfaced his craft at mid-day in broad daylight and fired a couple of torpedoes. No damage was done, and the escorts on the starboard flank gave him a good run for his money!

We were now at action stations each night from dusk until daylight, and although the night of the 9th and the following day
passed quietly, another attack took place on the night of the
10th and a further ship was destroyed with loss of 38 lives,
15 survivors out of 53 being picked up by the *Godetia*. 11th
January saw the arrival of assistance we had so urgently needed.
We were joined by a Support Group consisting of the destroyers
Quiberon, *Penn* and *Pathfinder*. We were now only three days'
sailing off Gibraltar and the rest of the trip passed quietly.

As the "Rock" loomed into sight on 14th January, all ratings
off watch were mustered on the boat-deck and briefed by the
Captain on the strict security to be observed on arrival. No details
of the trip whatsoever were to be divulged to anyone – where we
had come from, how many ships we had started with, etc. etc.
As we drew nearer, signals flashed to and from the shore station,
and as our two remaining ships were taken over by the destroyers, we were instructed to go alongside the Admiralty oiler lying
at anchor, and "top up" before entering harbour. This we did,
and much to our surprise we were given all the details we were to
keep so secret about, and even more, for they knew the name of
the German commander who had led the U-boats into battle. A
full report had already been broadcast over German radio.[5]

Few men aboard ship in a convoy were sanguine about the
prospect of crossing the Atlantic. They knew that enemy submarines might follow them for days, waiting until an entire pack
had assembled before attacking. Since these attacks almost always
came at night, every dusk must have brought a sense of dread.
Sometimes this was thankfully misplaced, as is shown by the
experience of one vessel:

A black, silky Caribbean night. No moon. Eagerly, keen eyes
scan the darkness for the source of that radar echo. Then, it's
there – a long, low, sinister shape, dead ahead, right across the
convoy's path. In that deathly quiet, sound travels easily, so
"Action Stations" is mounted in silence.

Then, shattering the dark of the night, a star shell from our
deck-gun. Now we see the enemy, in sharp silhouette against the
glare of the starshell bursts. About 200 feet long with the hump
of a conning-tower amidships.

Silence is abandoned as Commander Fitzgerald decides to save his ammo and gives the order "Stand by to ram!" We on the after gun-deck, never having seen a ramming, much less taken part in one, ignore the instructions to lie down, feet forward, and all of us stare ahead towards that shape. Suddenly, a shout from the bridge and the ship heels hard a-starboard.

We later found that the black shape was in fact the island of La Sola and we had been saved from a nasty crumpling of the bows by the sharp eyes of the quartermaster, who had hauled the wheel hard over without waiting for an order. Back aft, we knew nothing of the reason for the sudden change, but the Petty Officer in charge of depth charges made his own mind up when he saw the dark shape sliding past and pulled a toggle, firing the port thrower. A charge flew through the air, bounced on the "conning tower", so close were we, rolled into the sea and exploded.

Though this was a false alarm, within twenty-four hours the danger was real enough. The following night,

[w]e had just come down to the mess at the end of the first dog-watch [from 4 to 6 p.m.] when the buzzers went, calling us to Action Stations. I flew up the ladders and as I reached the well-deck, I saw the ship on our port side suddenly vanish behind a huge cloud of brown smoke. I kept on running and when I reached the after gun-deck, about 200 feet away, she had gone completely, yet her crew all got away. This was the Belgian *Bruxelles* and at the same time the US tanker *Franklin K Lane* was hit and went on fire.

We dropped a lot of high explosive, but with doubtful results. Commander "Fitz" decided it was his duty to steam round the burning tanker for three hours, in case we had missed any survivors, and our hearts thumped as we imagined the sort of target we must present against the bright flames . . . .[6]

Even in daylight a crew would be jittery, as a West Indian merchant seaman remembered. The sight of drifting debris from other vessels was bound to be sobering:

That year whilst in the Mona passage we encountered a wooden hull floating submerged with several rafts floating in the vicinity. There were neither bodies nor signs of survivors. I realized then that we were in the thick of things and pondered my own mortality!

Several months later off the coast of Puerto Rico at around midday alarm bells sounded and all hands were on deck and at respective boat stations with life-jackets, blankets and food. A periscope had been sighted following us. We increased our speed from 9 to 15 knots and remained on full alert for four hours. After this incident a naval ship always escorted us.[7]

A St Lucian merchant sailor had a very similar experience:

While other ships of the Merchant Marine travelled in convoys we travelled escorted continuously by torpedo boats. Our work was the repair of submarine communication cables. There were anxious moments. Many times we encountered floating ships' masts, wreckage and floating lifeboats from sunken ships. Never a survivor did we meet! On one occasion we were alerted by an alarm from the crow's nest to the presence of a submarine astern, following us. Each man found his station at his respective life-boat. The Captain proceeded on a zigzag course across the open ocean and the attendant torpedo boat was alerted causing it to make several sweeps of the surrounding areas. We remained alert at our stations from mid-day for the next four hours when we got the all-clear. Men prayed as never before, yet no one panicked.[8]

All those who experienced an attack by torpedoes remembered exactly where they were when the dreaded moment came, and most had at least some memory of the aftermath. The circumstances could differ widely – some were in the balmy Caribbean while others were in the freezing waters of the North Atlantic – but the horror was the same. A Barbadian on his way to Canada also saw the telltale debris that indicated U-boats in the vicinity. He was soon to become one of their victims.

Two days out from Bermuda, all sorts of wreckage could be seen floating on the surface of the sea – tables, chairs, mattresses and things from sunken ships that could float on water.

I walked into the [ship's] library where one of the stewards was printing menus for the next day. I looked at the map of Canada and the Caribbean. I was trying to figure out our distance from

Canada when suddenly there was a terrific explosion. The lights went out. At 10.00 p.m. a torpedo had struck the ship. The ship immediately leaned to one side and became filled with smoke and fumes. It was dark and I could not find my way out no matter how hard I tried.

In sheer desperation, I flung myself down and to my surprise found that I had thrown myself through a doorway. This led to a long passageway.

He followed the passageway and reached the deck, but his problems were by no means over:

The deck of the ship being slanted and wet, I slid and struck my head against the railing of the ship. I lost consciousness and was lying there when suddenly a big wave washed over me. I jumped up and realized I was still alive, but still in danger. Someone shouted above and looking up I saw Kite Hamblin, one of the fifty Barbadians. He was laden with life belts and he threw one in my direction.

He and the other survivors managed to board a lifeboat and attempted to pull away from the vessel. About two hundred yards away,

[w]e stopped and looked at the ship but immediately there was a loud explosion and a tremendous flash and the two ends of the ship could be seen pointing against a dark sombre sky. We did not have much time to reflect on this, because suddenly a great beam of light appeared out of the water. Gradually it dawned that it was a submarine. "Down! Down! Flat in the boat!" shouted our officer. We immediately lounged flat in the bottom of the boat. "They going to riddle us with machine-gun bullets," said one person. The light played on us for a short time then the submarine turned and sped away. "They only taking pictures," said the officer.[9]

It was three days before they were rescued. A British Merchant Navy officer, aboard a vessel in convoy, was about to go to bed when

I heard a thud. At first it sounded like a depth charge. I then felt a series of vibrations which had a decided familiarity about them. I knew that something was decidedly amiss, and from past experience began quickly to realize that the ship had been hit by either a torpedo or a bomb. I began to rush over towards my bunk when all the lights went out. Not unreasonably there was a certain amount of confusion and very quickly I learned that sea water was flooding the engine-room. Then there was another explosion, but this time it was from another ship which had been torpedoed. As we were obviously still afloat, I found it difficult to actually believe that we had been hit, or that we were sinking.

The U-boat attack on the convoy began just after midnight on 17th August. At the time we were in the channel between Jamaica and Haiti and only 160 miles from Guantanamo which is on the southern end of Cuba. We abandoned ship by climbing rope ladders down to the lifeboats. Our ship, hardly a week old, stayed afloat for about two hours before it began to gradually sink, sliding bow-first until it disappeared out of sight forever. Day-break came and with it a Royal Navy corvette which stopped to pick us all up. We were taken on to Guantanamo.[10]

In a convoy from New York was a group of West Indians on their way to work in industry in Britain. One of them remembered the stricken feeling when the escorts were withdrawn and the loneliest part of the ocean lay ahead. He was right to fear the coming nights.

After two days and nights, the aeroplanes and corvettes ran out of distance. They could go no further and so the convoy was left with nothing but the clear blue skies above and the rolling waves of the Atlantic Ocean.

On the third night, at 10.00 p.m. exactly, the U-boat struck amongst the ships of the convoy. There were loud explosions and the sky was lit up like an inferno. By daybreak, there was silence and the damage done was quite visible. There were now vast gaps in the convoy. There were broken and battered ships scattered about. However, the ships which were intact kept moving steadily ahead throughout the daytime. They just sailed ahead and, as before, 10.00 p.m. in the night, the U-boats struck and again there were explosions, "Boom! Bang!" The skies were again lit up all red and smoky, with the occasional flashes of fire from the explosions. This again continued until daylight.

On the third night at 10.00 p.m. the same destructive chorus opened up with the usual sounds and the heavens blazing red from the fires on the sea. As the stricken ships exploded one ship spilled the liquid all over [the sea] and as it became alight the ships were all travelling through waves of flaming fire. The sea was so brilliantly lit that the whole scene was like a well-lit stage. The crew on board a burning ship formed a queue and the priest placed the Holy Sacrament into each man's mouth, made the sign of the cross, then each man, after he had taken the Sacrament, jumped overboard right into the flames. The priest was last man; he also swallowed the Sacrament then, clasping his hands together, he too dived into the flames . . . .[11]

A British Honduras forester on his way to Britain experienced attack "one bleak and misty October day" in northern waters. On this occasion, however, the tables were turned:

Without any warning we received one almighty blow to the port side. A torpedo had landed smack amidships. All hell broke

Explosion of an oil tanker in the Caribbean after being torpedoed by a U-boat. (Imperial War Museum, Misc. 51235.)

loose! The ship began to heel over fast, the lights went out in our cabins and all over the ship; there was a scramble for the nearest exit. Life jackets were hurriedly put on. Most of us carried out this intricate manoeuvre while at the same time making for the first exit we could find. In the general panic, I could find neither my boots nor get into my life jacket fast enough. We believed we were going to end up in the icy water. Finally, we managed to reach the upper deck and ran for our respective life-boat stations.

We were to spend many hours on deck, in northern ice-berg waters, while the search for the U-boat went on. The warning whistle on other ships could be heard as well as that on our own. To our relief, the ship had ceased to keel over. It continued to list badly, at about twenty degrees, but was capable of going on slowly provided the engines could carry her along. It was fortunate that the torpedo had not hit the engine-room in the stern. Everywhere was wild activity. Escort vessels were rushing here and there, dropping depth charges and emitting their doleful hooting-whistling sound as they went about protecting the main body of the convoy.

The submarine had half-surfaced after the depth charge explosions and our guns kept up the attack, firing until at long last we sank the sub. A puff of whitish smoke went up, and down to the bottom of the Atlantic she went! Her crew abandoned ship, and we rescued the survivors. The deck hands, our lads, everybody was shouting for joy! At the same time, there were cries for the prisoners to be handed over to the howling crew: "Give us the b——s!, Give us the b——s!" But soon they were below, out of sight, captives on a ship they almost sank.[12]

When a ship was hit, a strict procedure had to be gone through, as much as time and circumstances permitted. *Empire Starling* was carrying a cargo of beef and butter picked up in Brazil and Argentina. On the evening of 21 November 1942 it had just reached the "Serpent's Mouth" – the entrance to the Gulf of Paria in Trinidad – when a torpedo found it. The captain, who had already been taking the necessary precautions, knew at once what to do:

At about 7.00 p.m., darkness having set in, I decided to do the required "evasive" steering, to shake off following submarines, and was going to alter the course 30 degrees to starboard for two hours. I left my cabin to go on the navigating bridge to make this course alteration, and had reached the bridge ladder, when the vessel shook violently and two blinding explosions occurred on the ship's port side. The shock to the ship threw me from the bottom steps of the ladder onto the deck, accompanied by flying pieces of wood and metal and a deluge of salt water. The ship took a sudden list to port of about fifteen degrees and stayed a while at that angle.

The *Empire Starling* had been hit by two torpedoes fired simultaneously and they had struck the vessel in the forward and after part of her hull, on the port side. It was too dark to see the submarine that had done the destruction, and I decided that it would be best to stand by in the lifeboats and if no other torpedo was fired in the course of some time we could, if the ship still floated, return on board and see what could be done to try and save her. We would at least have the gun aft to reply, if the submarine came within sight of us.

After throwing the weighted bag over the side and getting rid of all secret papers, I made for the boat deck and gave orders for the crew to take to the boats and stand by one ship's length astern. On going to the radio room, the Operator informed me that he had got away the S.O.S. twice on the emergency set – the main set aerial had been carried away by the shock of the explosions. He was told to get into the lifeboat that had the wireless set in it.

The Chief Officer and Chief Steward informed me that all their staffs were mustered and getting away in the boats. The Radio Operator had thrown the radio codes and secret orders over the side and the Chief Officer informed me that two naval gunners, on watch aft on the gun platform, had been thrown from the platform down onto the poop deck by the explosion. Both were injured and were placed in the boats before lowering into the water.

Before leaving the ship, I decided to go to the crews' quarters forward, amidships and aft and to shout for anyone who might have gone unnoticed in the muster for the lifeboats. There was no response to my shouting, and all secrets and codes being disposed of, I made my way to the lifeboat that was left alongside in the water, the others being astern of the ship at this time. There were four lifeboats on the *Empire Starling*, and all got clear of the ship, though difficulty was experienced with the boats on the starboard side as the vessel now had a good list, judged to be about 25 degrees, and over to port. After getting into the lifeboat we shipped oars and rowed astern of the ship. On reaching about 200 feet from the ship, there was another terrific explosion on the port side of the ship, as the submarine put in another torpedo to finish the ship off. In the blinding flash there was no view of the submarine, and we felt a violent gust of wind and a deluge of sea-water that drenched everyone in the boat. Within about two minutes after the ship had received the third torpedo, she turned quickly over to port and rolled down into the sea, with a dying hiss of steam. All the boats were collected together, then a start was made to steer a course for the West Indian islands, some three to four hundred miles away . . . .[13]

Sometimes the victim of a torpedo attack could sound remarkably laconic, as did a seaman interviewed by the *Barbados Advocate* following his rescue. The chief officer of *Scottish Star* told the newspaper's readers:

I had just come off watch and was enjoying a beer when I heard two explosions. It was very unexpected because I had thought we were outside the danger zone. The submarine had cut across our bows. We had plenty of time and so I finished my beer. We had four boats, which seemed adequate for the 72 members of the crew. We remained in the vicinity of the ship all night and [then] steered due west for Barbados.[14]

That was all very well provided one had a comfortable boat and some provisions. A sailor involved in rescuing survivors described a scene in which their troubles were clearly not over:

At last we sighted one stricken ship, and as we drew nearer we saw a sight I shall never forget – a whole fleet of ships' lifeboats, each with a pair of bright red sails, bobbing about in the water, and each one packed with survivors. There was no land in sight and it can be imagined how glad those men were to see us arrive on the scene. There are some pretty nasty fish in those waters too – we saw "barracuda" fish jumping out of the water and snapping their jaws like dogs alongside one of our boats, and the occupants were hitting out at them with pieces of wood![15]

For those out at sea who managed to escape a sinking ship and were not drenched in burning oil, there was the prospect of days spent clinging to wreckage – suffering thirst and burns – in waters patrolled by sharks and barracuda. Nevertheless, some survivors displayed remarkable coolness when rescue arrived, as can be seen from this report in the *Barbados Advocate*: "Yesterday the fishing-boat '*Stella*' towed into the Careenage a lifeboat with sixteen survivors of the Blue Star Line steamer '*Scottish Star*', 7,224 tons gross, which had been torpedoed on Thursday about 650 miles east of Barbados."[16]

Notwithstanding these unemotional and rather relaxed accounts by those who had survived sinking, the ordeals suffered by hundreds of seamen drifting in lifeboats or rafts, or just clinging to bits of wreckage, were horrific. The plight of those who managed to reach safety shocked the islanders and brought home to them the reality of the war being waged around them. It also presented their local medical services, the Red Cross, the St John Ambulance and similar caring organizations with an unexpected challenge.

Life in the islands was affected also when, as often happened, U-boats surfaced and destroyed with gunfire the schooners on which the inter-island trade depended. This led not only to injuries or death for local West Indian crewmembers, but also to the rationing of some commodities.

Prior to 1942 the convoy system was not fully developed and the shortage of Allied ships made the task more difficult. Even when this situation improved, most of the ships were deployed to carry "war cargoes", and as a result many bypassed the islands in the Caribbean. This caused great scarcity until a new system was introduced by way of creating central distribution areas (Trinidad supplied Barbados and the neighbouring Leeward and Windward islands) and greater use of schooners for inter-island traffic. This increasingly led to schooners becoming the targets of U-boats. *Mona Marie*, a Barbadian schooner commanded by Captain Laurie Hassell, for example, was intercepted by U-126 (commanded by

The schooner *Mona Marie*, which was lost through U-boat action in June 1942. (Photo by Captain Laurie Hassell in Warren Alleyne, *Barbados at War, 1939–1945* [Barbados: Warren Alleyne, 1999].)

Kapitänleutnant Ernst Bauer) with a burst of machine-gun fire and later shelled. The crew of *Mona Marie* survived and later reached Mustique, in the Grenadines.

By 1942 the West Indies Schooner Pool Authority had been established, with headquarters in Barbados, which resulted in a more efficient method of distribution. Cargo ships would unload their goods at key ports according to their final destination. Local schooners would then speedily take these consignments to their final destination. The members of the pool were mostly private owners, as well as the governments of the Leeward and Windward islands, Barbados, Trinidad and Tobago and British Guiana.

More than seven thousand seamen died in Caribbean waters. From Barbados alone seventy-four men were lost at sea (their names are inscribed on a memorial in Bridgetown's Military Cemetery that was recently dedicated in their honour). A large number of West Indians who had volunteered for war service joined the Canadian and British merchant navies. After the war it was calculated that the casualty rate in the US merchant navy exceeded that of the armed services – 17 per cent of all merchant seamen as opposed to 9 per cent of those in the navy, marines, army and air force.

But what of the opponents in this conflict – the U-boat crews who came to know Caribbean waters so well and to wreak such destruction among the convoys? What was it like to sail on these missions, to live in claustrophobic silence beneath the surface and to strike from the darkness at fellow sailors and their vessels? Through an extraordinary circumstance we have been able to find out. Captain Monkton of *Empire Starling*, the sinking of which was described earlier, became a German prisoner when the U-boat surfaced and took him on board. He then travelled all the way back to Europe in the company of the men who had killed many of his crew. He wrote a memoir of this experience which has never been published previously, and in which he portrays life aboard U-163. He begins by describing the boat's interior and its living conditions:

> I was given a berth-bed in the Officers quarters, which quarters also served as a dining mess and recreation room for the Commander and Officers. This berth was forward of the control room which was directly under the conning tower, and it had four "tip-up" bunks, which when not in use could be tipped up vertically to the side of the submarine. On one side, for meals the upper bed was canted up to the ships side, and the lower bed served as a settle seat for the collapsible table that was fitted up, the other seating being stools of a collapsible type. Along the starboard side throughout the length of the submarine was the working alleyway, being the only passageway from forward to aft. I noticed that when any of the crew passed through the Officers berth, they always raised their hands in the Nazi salute.
>
> Throughout the whole of my passage on the U-163, which I learned was the number of the submarine, the food consisted of soups, sausages, liverwurst, tinned fruits and vegetables. We got meat later on when the U-163 was re-supplied near the Bay of Biscay by a submarine tanker, and then only sufficient to last for two days. When I arrived on board there were some

potatoes, about half a ton at the most, and stored underneath the navigating table in the control room under the conning tower. These potatoes lasted only a few days as the Germans did not show any knowledge of how to preserve them. When they started to go bad they bucketed them up to the harbour deck while they were proceeding on the surface, washed them in salt water and then restowed them in the locker. Within two days there was a smell of bad fish about the potatoes and they had all gone rotten. The food was all tinned and the products mostly of Portugal, Italy, France and Denmark, to whom the crew used to refer to as "our *kamarads*", but in my estimation of the first two countries, just rats to be trading with a country that was doing so much harm and whose ideals were so foreign to them.

The small kitchen for cooking the meals was forward of the Officers' quarters and was of very limited space but fitted with electric stove and oven, electric water boiler, and the usual pantry washing equipment.

The Commander's room was a curtained-off room with bed, writing desk and dressing table. Opposite his quarters were the Radio and Asdic rooms and a store-room. This accommodation was between the control room and the Officers' quarters.

Fresh water was scarce and obtained from two-gallon-size storage canisters, the distilling plant of the submarine being out of commission. Personal washing was done from a basin-compactum on a bulkhead of the Officers' quarters, seawater and a special salt-water soap being used, a very poor wash and lather being obtained from this. Salt-water soap has always been a very poor substitute for ordinary soap and fresh water for personal washing; nothing very effective having been found to decently take the place of ordinary soap, which of course, cannot be used with sea water.

He then moved on to the boat's armament:

The U-163 had four torpedo tubes forward and two aft, was about 285 feet in length, carried a crew of 40 men and was commissioned at Kiel in 1940. She had been running out of the French West Coast ports since Germany had occupied them. The crew seemed to be very young fellows of about 18 to 25

years of age, with the exception of two Warrant Officers, the
Captain and the Doctor.

And he noticed the unhealthy appearance of the crew:

All the crew seemed to be affected with constant boils on some
part of their body, and many with swollen feet and legs, being
the forerunner of kidney trouble, and the curing of this trouble
would be difficult under the conditions the German submarine
crews endured, unless reasonable rest at the end of each commission could be given.

The most difficult part of Captain Monkton's situation was
having to watch powerlessly as the submarine attacked Allied
shipping:

Throughout the day, the U-163 cruised on a southeasterly course
and at about 4 p.m. a ship was sighted. I was below at the time
and the Oberleutnant was hurriedly called and orders were
shouted all through the ship by their speaker-repeaters. Speed
was increased judging by the increased vibration throughout the
submarine. No-one was allowed on deck and the course altered
by the movement of the ship in the seaway. Varying courses and
speeds were made and at about 6.30 p.m. when the Unterleutnant
passed through the officers quarters, [he] informed me that they
were going to submerge to periscope depth to torpedo another
ship, nationality unknown. It was my first experience of diving
in a submarine and beyond the angle of the dive, it was not
alarming.

At about 6.45 p.m. I heard the torpedo being fired, the hiss
caused by the compressed air used to initially send out the
torpedo, causing a definite pressure on the ear drums. Less
than a minute after the torpedo had been fired, I heard a slight
"ping", as the torpedo struck the ship. Later, I learned that two
torpedoes had been fired simultaneously. About ten minutes
after the firing of the torpedoes, the submarine broke surface,
and apparently headed down towards the scene of destruction.
From below I heard repeated calls of "what ship" and "where is
the captain". No reply was heard by me and some five minutes
later I heard the "rat-tat" of about 30 rounds of machine-gun
firing, followed in the distance by screams and cries.

The ship had apparently been Brazilian, and one survivor was brought aboard from a lifeboat to be questioned, but the submarine commander "would not take the person from the boat prisoner, as he was a Negro and they did not like them".

The tension and brutality of these moments was balanced by long days of routine:

> Life went on in the submarine, day by day, with the usual monotony, practice diving being carried out every two days, these "crash dives" being carried out at different times during the days and the submarine remaining under the water for about three or four hours at a depth of about 20 metres (60 feet). The weather was continuously bad with a fresh S.E. breeze and rough seas, the submarine always having seas strike the forward part of the conning tower when running on the surface and the overdeck always awash.

Monkton heard an interesting compliment to the RAF:

> The U-163 was successful in torpedoing two American tanker steamers off the US coast. Eventually, she worked her way into the Caribbean Sea, evading several attacks from American aircraft. They seemed to look upon the American navy and air force with contempt as they maintained that they were nowhere near as effective and dangerous as the British Navy and RAF. They were very scared of their passage through the Bay of Biscay and of sighting the patrolling Sunderlands.

And he witnessed a near-disaster for the submarine:

> During the month of October 1942, the U-163 lay off the entrance to Wilhelmstadt in Curaçao, off the coast of Venezuela, and as a convoy of tankers left that harbour under US destroyer escort she had three successes. The convoy was coming out of the harbour, and after they had cleared the entrance, a destroyer of the *Anson* type was torpedoed and set on fire fore and aft and two of the escorting tankers were also torpedoed. The submarine was, worse luck, nearly turned over by the striking of the conning tower by a ship of the convoy that tried to ram her, as she was submerging from her periscope depth. The submarine heeled over to an alarming angle but she managed to right herself and go down deep.

Captain Monkton made several observations on life aboard:

> Every night at a certain time, the U-163 was in touch with Berlin and other German wireless stations, and if not on the surface could from periscope depth run up the 36-foot retractable tapered aerial which was mounted on the deck of the conning tower, and so received orders for her next day's operating area. The charts used on the U-163 were all marked out in numbered squares for easy reference and signalling purposes. The depth recorders were marked to 200 metres and we only went down to that depth once while I was aboard. The usual practice "crash" dive was of 20 metres approx.
>
> All the ratings were very good at signalling with flags and Morse lamp and all very good at steering the ship with the electric control handles. The ship's cook was supposed to be a good cook and baker, but he had no opportunity to exhibit his knowledge as all he did was to open the tins of products and make the contents into soup.

And he described the hunt for prey:

> On about 4th December, 1942, the U-163 was cruising on her easterly course and about 200 miles north of Georgetown, as far as I could gather. At about two p.m. an American cruiser and an accompanying destroyer were sighted on the bow. The U-163 dived hurriedly to periscope depth and closed in for action, everyone on board being chased to their attack stations. The stern torpedo tubes were to be used and the U-163 placed stern on to the approaching cruiser, the propeller just being kept turning over slowly to keep steerage way on the submarine. All electric fans in the submarine were turned off and amongst the crew there was great tension and excitement. I, of course, hoped that the cruiser would alter course away and so fool them, for she would surely be going at a good speed, perhaps much more than the U-163 could muster at top speed on the surface, which was 21 knots.
>
> The heat inside the submarine was unbearable and the perspiration just poured off me in streams. I had been told that I had to remain in the Officers' quarters during the action and could only surmise what was taking place, until I heard the story afterwards. All was deathly silent, except for the occasional sharp

orders through the repeaters which were placed in each compartment of the hull.

Nothing happened for a long while and I did not hear the hiss of the torpedoes being sent on their path of destruction. Later, the U-163 took on a "down by the head" position and it was evident that we were diving deeper, also the engine movement could be heard as if they were being used also. Some ten minutes after this, I could hear a noise like the rush of an express train and then the explosion of the "ashcans" raining down with their explosions and severe shakings of the U-163. We remained very quiet and still for about an hour, the explosions having died away for a long period, and there having been six of them altogether. After remaining still and quiet for several hours and the hot atmosphere inside the U-163 being just unbearable we rose to periscope depth and after a careful look round through the two periscopes and seeing nothing, the Commander broke surface with the U-163. The change of air was most noticeable, even though I was not allowed on deck for some hours afterwards, the crew going up first.[17]

The U-boats began and ended their Caribbean sorties in the Bay of Biscay and the French Atlantic ports. After a lengthy patrol the crew looked forward to the sight of the French coast as proof that they had survived another patrol. When reaching the area, U-564, the vessel commanded by Kapitänleutnant Suhren, went through the customary procedures:

Suhren's conning-tower became crowded with men eager for a glimpse of the French landscape. Tightly coiled victory pennants, painstakingly hand-painted during the boredom of the return journey, were attached to the head of the retracted attack periscope, waiting for the grand unfurling. Atop the tube were also two crossed swords, made within the workshop, that graced the forward end of the diesel room and were designed to celebrate Suhren's award [the Knight's Cross].

Beneath a brilliant blue sky, the convoy headed east toward Brest. As the Rade de Brest enveloped U-564 within its beautiful rocky coastline, the periscope was extended and nine victory pennants fluttered proudly above the heads of the victorious crew. Lining both edges of the entrance channel to Brest lay

German U-boats abandoned at the Blohm and Voss shipyard in Hamburg, 4 May 1945. (Imperial War Museum, BU5290.)

heavy concrete bunkers, containing the large-calibre weapons of the coastal artillery, their crews emerging to wave to the small group of vessels welcoming the U-boat crew home. The curious mixture of medieval, Napoleonic and German fortresses lay on either flank of U-564 as she entered the Goulet de Brest, the slim channel that provided such excellent shelter and protected access to Brest's military harbour. More squat concrete shelters housed torpedo tubes that guarded the narrowest point of the Goulet, vessels being obliged to travel along two distinct marked channels. A small launch approached U-564, and several fellow-officers of the First U-boat Flotilla came aboard the boat, accompanied by Dr Richter, the flotilla's surgeon. The state of Suhren's men after seventy days at sea impressed Richter. They had lost little weight and appeared groomed and healthy to his brief spot checks.[18]

Suhren's men were fortunate in more than their state of health. Their return to port was uneventful and they were able to enjoy the traditional welcome from brass bands, pretty nurses and senior officers on the quay. The Allies were well aware that boats returning from the Caribbean had to cross that small and easily reconnoitred stretch of water, and it was therefore there that the Allies hunted them with especial vigour. The last of Captain Monkton's experiences aboard U-163 was an attack by a British aircraft.

On January 4th, at about 4 p.m. a sudden crash dive was made due to an RAF aircraft being sighted on the port bow. The RAF aircraft had also sighted us, as we were soon to know. We went on down to some 120 metres and continued on slowly, with some short periods of stoppages. The under-water bombs came down, and the RAF must have had some good explosive to drop, as the U-163 just shook and rattled with the "ashcans" about 1000 metres off, according to what the Officers told me. Still, the RAF did not score a hit that time, and we ran on for a long period under the surface.

There was no doubt that the Nazis were very scared of the RAF and for two reasons. They were so quick at following up any trace of a submarine and holding on to it with relays of aircrafts or with the assistance of a naval craft if there was one about in the vicinity, and their periodical operations of laying acoustic mines off the leading-in lanes from the sea to the French ports. The U-163 was not de-gaussed [demagnetized] for mine purposes, and I was told that they had lost many a submarine entering or leaving the French ports even when submerged. The effect of the RAF's efficiency was very shaking to the submarine crew's morale, for they dreaded their passages across the Bay of Biscay and into and from their French Bases.[19]

Extraordinarily, at the end of the voyage, as Monkton was awaiting transport to a prison camp, both the commander and the boat's doctor gave him their home addresses and said that they would welcome a letter from him if they could do anything to help. Somewhat churlishly perhaps, in view of this kindness, he threw the addresses overboard.

The End in Sight

The U-boat campaign, which included activity in the Mediterranean, Baltic and Arctic seas and off the coasts of Africa as well as in the North Atlantic and Caribbean, did not end suddenly or spectacularly. Gradually, however, the Allies became better at defending themselves. They increased the number of escort vessels and observation posts. Better coordination developed between the British and American navies. The greatly increased use of aircraft (some of which were specially adapted for attacking U-boats), based either in Iceland or on carriers, meant that Allied patrols could cover the entire North and mid-Atlantic; they sank a concentration of "milk cows" (returning boats) off the Azores. The Bay of Biscay remained a fearsome killing-ground as bombers hunted submarines in this comparatively small area. The Atlantic convoys were more heavily guarded by escorts, and Allied intelligence became more accurate. For U-boat crews the "happy times" were a thing of the past. In May 1943 forty-one U-boats, many with inexperienced crews, were lost, and Dönitz decided to waste no further lives in mass attacks there. The Battle of the Atlantic was officially ended.

In that long, decisive struggle the naval and air forces of the Allies had at last gained the upper hand. Nor were they to lose it. Dönitz's hopes of renewing his campaign with large-scale operations in other areas had been dashed. Hitler ordered that the U-boats be directed against Allied shipping involved from November 1942 onwards in Operation *Torch*, the Anglo-American landings in French North Africa and the subsequent invasions of Sicily and Italy. But the fundamental factor that conquered the U-boat menace was the huge advances in science and technology made under the stimulus of war. In the application of radar, the detection of U-boats both surfaced and submerged, the coordination of sea and air operations, the production of more effective weaponry – in the whole field of submarine warfare – Allied technology outpaced the Germans'. Moreover, the industrial might of the United States dwarfed that of German-occupied Europe. When the Second World War ended,

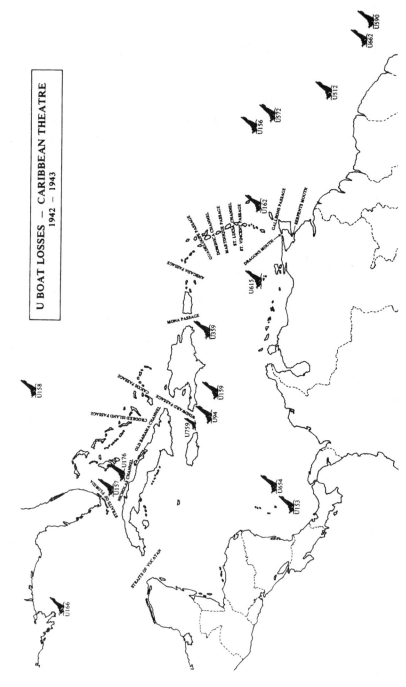

U-boat losses in 1942–1943. (Gaylord Kelshall, *The U-Boat War in the Caribbean* [Shrewsbury, UK: Airlife, 1994].)

the industrial output of that nation was greater than that of the rest of the world put together, and it was the most efficient.

Nevertheless, offensive operations continued with improved submarines (types XXI and XXIII could travel farther and stay submerged for longer and were equipped with better torpedoes, radar and anti-aircraft weapons), but their crews found it increasingly difficult to attack without being detected. Losses continued to mount – fifty-four U-boats were lost in June and July – and an attempt to find softer targets off the South American coast was foiled when Brazil declared war on Germany. At the end of 1943 more than 160 U-boats were still operational. The Caribbean had seen the sinking of 36 per cent of all the merchant shipping lost that year, but this was not enough to impede the ceaseless flow of traffic across the Atlantic. The German boats no longer sought to make concerted attacks; their purpose now was to create the greatest possible nuisance and tie down as much of the Allies' resources as they could. Shipyards in Germany could not replace losses or introduce new types quickly enough to have any hope of winning the sea war, although, had the newest types appeared sooner and in larger numbers, they would have prolonged it.

An Anglo-American invasion of north-west Europe was looming and U-boats were needed there. They played a part during Operation *Overlord* in June 1944 but had no influence on the outcome. The subsequent liberation of France by the Allies deprived the German navy of its bases on the Atlantic and severely restricted its vessels' access to the Western Hemisphere. The demise of Vichy France had already meant the end of pro-Axis government in the French islands and the subsequent loss to the Germans of facilities there used by U-boat crews.

Nevertheless, it is worth remembering that the U-boats were never entirely defeated. Operating from their remaining ports in Norway and Germany and using a greatly improved snorkel apparatus, they continued to fight the war. U-boats could still roam the world's greatest oceans at will. Snorkels and the practice of never using radio during a patrol enabled them to remain submerged and undetected for lengthy periods. As Gaylord Kelshall explains in his seminal work on the Caribbean war,

[t]he crew could rely on the fact that they were virtually immune from attack. The types of radar used in the Caribbean could detect a snorkelling operation only under the most favourable circumstances. There were numerous sightings and anti-submarine attacks, against driftwood, wreckage, whitecaps and whales. It was very frustrating because the Americans could not attack the U-boats until they detected them and they could only detect them after they attacked something.[20]

From the summer of 1944 the area of ocean designated by the United States as the Caribbean Defence Command was extended to a point fifteen hundred miles east of the island chain, and a vaster section of the Atlantic became the responsibility of the US Navy. American forces in the Caribbean began to dismantle their defences, and in the autumn ships ceased to observe a blackout when at sea. In December the carrier USS *Randolph* crossed the Gulf of Mexico without an escort – an event that would have been unthinkable a year previously.

But it was not quite over. Though U-boats had not operated in large numbers in the Caribbean since the summer of 1944, two boats, U-516 and U-532, which had set out from Norway, shadowed a convoy and torpedoed the tanker *Harrisburg* off Haiti. This was the last sinking in the region. As the war in Europe ended, two U-boats, U-530 and U-977, well stocked with fuel and rations and equipped with the latest snorkel device, sailed from Germany and reached Argentina some ten weeks later. There they surrendered to the local authorities in hopes of a comfortable internment, but they were handed over to the Americans as prisoners of war. Their long, silent journey to South America gave birth to ill-founded rumours that they had been carrying senior Nazi party officials, such as Martin Bormann, who were wanted by the victorious Allies as war criminals.

The sinking of *Harrisburg* had brought the number of Allied merchantmen lost in the Caribbean to four hundred, just over 15 per cent of their total shipping losses worldwide. In comparison, German casualties in the region had been slight: only seventeen U-boats had been lost there. This was a mere 2 per cent of the overall losses suffered by the U-boat arm.

PART 4

The Remnants of Five Hundred Years of War and Conflict

CHAPTER 16
The Caribbean Legacy

Federation, independence, regionalization, economic progress and the impact on Britain.

The British Empire had survived the war without loss of territory, and the human cost of victory, though grievous, was far less than in 1918.

But the economic cost had been huge – the war deprived Britain of much of its reserves. Between 1939 and 1945 the country lost a quarter of its stored wealth, as well as nearly 70 per cent of its export trade. To compensate, a loan of $375 million was requested from the United States. This was granted, at 2 per cent interest, in December 1945.

In 1945 Britain found itself a debtor nation; it still had the largest empire, but the world was dominated by two superpowers, the United States and the Soviet Union. The United States was the mightier of the two; its supremacy would be confirmed in 1989 when the Soviet satellite empire of communist-led states in Eastern Europe collapsed and the USSR itself dissolved. In 1945 the United States enjoyed the same international pre-eminence that Britain had in 1815.

As soon as the war ended, the European overseas empires began to unravel. In the Far East, Japan's swift seizure of large territories had undermined local peoples' trust and respect for the colonial powers, and their experience fighting the Japanese had given them skills and weaponry that could now be used against their former rulers. Long guerrilla campaigns began in Indonesia, Malaya and French Indo-China that would mean years of instability and strife. In the Middle East Palestine became a thorn in the side of its British administrators as Jews fought to establish a homeland in Arab lands.

Table 16.1: Casualties of the Second World War

	Dead	Missing	Wounded
Great Britain	233,042	57,472	275,975
Canada	36,018	2,866	53,073
Australia	21,415	6,519	37,477
New Zealand	9,844	2,201	19,253
South Africa	6,417	1,980	13,773
India	23,925	12,264	62,064
Colonies	6,741	14,811	6,773

Source: Lawrence James, *The Rise and Fall of the British Empire* (London: Little, Brown, 1994).

Other colonies pursued a more ordered path to independence. India, with the potential to be a major power in its own right, was impatient to cut its ties with Britain. It did so in August 1947, even though the speed of its political change led to partitioning of the subcontinent and to tensions that have continued ever since. Ceylon (now Sri Lanka) became a nation in 1948, and Burma in 1949. British governments both Labour and Conservative sought to grant self-government responsibly, allowing colonies time to establish democracy and to train a governing class, but in 1957, with the independence of Ghana – a country not at all prepared to take over its destiny – the floodgates opened. Throughout Africa and Asia colonies scrambled for independence whether or not they were ready.

Britain had been impoverished by the conflict and was struggling to pay for its newborn welfare state. The postwar Labour government, which was sympathetic to decolonization, had been anxious to offload the expensive responsibilities of colonial power but was now burdened with the expense of being a major player in the Cold War. Many in Westminster thus shared the feelings of colonial peoples – feelings vociferously championed in Washington, DC – that independence should come sooner rather than later. For these reasons the situation in the West Indies at the end of the Second World War bore no relation to that of a generation earlier. In 1918, despite discontent, there had been no question of the region's seeking autonomy from Britain. Now it seemed clear that significant changes were on the way.

Society within the islands had also changed considerably. The wartime presence of thousands of Americans had altered the cultural balance, and many West Indians now felt they had more in common with the United States and Canada than with Britain. Other factors were also in play. By 1945 Jamaica, for instance, was a very different place from the colony it had been a decade earlier. Bauxite, of which the island possessed the world's largest deposits, was creating wealth on a scale not seen since the heyday of sugar. Jamaica and Trinidad were industrializing rapidly and a coloured middle class had developed. Tourism was on the increase as the islands gained popularity with the international rich. Jamaica had a modernized constitution, held democratic elections and had, in Norman Manley and Alexander Bustamante, leaders of extraordinary charisma. Though they differed, both had the vision, the ability and the popularity to lead the country to independence and to found a new nation. A palpable sense of confidence had developed.

Britain was willing to grant independence in the Caribbean, but was sceptical of the smaller islands' ability to form viable nations. The answer was federation, an idea previously considered in 1871 and 1936. Now it was discussed at conferences in Jamaica (1947) and London (1953). The proposed economic and political community of territories would include the islands and the two mainland colonies, British Honduras and British Guiana. The federation would have dominion status, with a single governor-general, and there would be a federal parliament in addition to the territories' own assemblies. As a first step towards integration, the University of the West Indies was founded in Jamaica in 1948.

Ten years later, on 3 January 1958, the Federation of the West Indies came into being, but it was in trouble from the very beginning.

The mainland territories had opted out and the community was therefore dominated by the largest islands – Jamaica and Trinidad – the latter having been chosen as home to the federal government. The islands had a long history of rivalry and mutual suspicion. Because they traditionally exported the same things – bananas and sugar – they were used to competing for both commerce and the aid they received from Britain. Communications between them were often poor, and many islands had more contact with London than with each other.

Trinidad and Jamaica had between them 70 per cent of the Federation's population, 80 per cent of its territory and three-quarters of its wealth, but these two major islands could not bury their rivalry. The smaller islands resented the overwhelming domination of the larger, while the larger islands felt that their economic progress was being slowed by the need to carry their less advanced neighbours. In 1960 the Jamaica Labour Party, led by Alexander Bustamante, adopted withdrawal from the Federation as its official policy. Norman Manley, his rival, had initially been enthusiastic, but he too decided that federation was a lost cause. He called a referendum on 19 September 1961 and the result left no doubt that the voting public wanted Jamaica to secede.

The Colonial Office also admitted defeat. Before the Federation was even officially wound up on 31 May 1962 – ironically, the day on which it had expected to formally join the Commonwealth – a Jamaican delegation visited London for talks on independence. For the large territories, and for many of the smaller ones, this was the only remaining option. Sir Kenneth Blackburn, the last governor of Jamaica, was later to comment:

> Our mistake is that we acted too fast in the establishment of the Federation, animated in part by the vapourings of the United Nations, in part by the desire of the British Treasury to rid itself of financial responsibilities overseas, and in part by the natural desire of West Indian leaders to control their own destinies. Although we had done much to promote regional collaboration, we should perhaps have been better advised to establish economic integration through a customs union before proceeding with political

federation. One is thankful that the wise West Indian leaders of today seem to be pursuing just this course. The establishment of a Caribbean Free Trade Area in 1968 and later of the Caribbean Community and Common Market are the first indigenously inspired attempt to promote genuine regional co-operation.[1]

With a future that promised excitement and rapid progress, memories of the Second World War faded quickly. The end of the war against Japan had meant loss of the Caribbean's strategic value (it was to be renewed, however, in 1959, when the Communist revolution in Cuba created a Cold War flashpoint, and in the early 1980s with the revolution in Grenada). The U-boat war also came to be forgotten beyond the seas where it had taken place. In view of its importance in terms of shipping sunk, this may seem surprising, but there were several reasons.

The U-boat war was largely overshadowed by events in other theatres. Understandably, public attention focussed mainly on Europe, while the Far Eastern war was symbolized by Midway, Burma and the Pacific islands. At sea the story of the Battle of the Atlantic, of which the Caribbean actions had been a part, was dominated by events taking place farther north. Between Canada and the United Kingdom, where the convoys assembled and made their crossings, were the scenes of greatest slaughter and greatest success. There ships ran the gauntlet of the largest wolf-packs, and that was where the greatest numbers of German boats had been destroyed. This conflict gripped people's imaginations and added to the prestige of American, British and Canadian sailors and airmen.

Those who sought to pick up the threads of their lives in the immediate aftermath of the war sometimes found themselves resented for having left their home environment while others had remained to keep the community ticking over. Louise Osbourne, for instance, resumed working for her old employer in St Lucia, but found that her wartime experiences were not an asset.

I worked at Barnard's Sons before going and I went to them and told them I'm back now, and I got the same job back but, of course, they were annoyed that I had left them, at all, to join the

ATS. They weren't as nice as when I first worked at Barnard's Sons, they were keeping up the idea that I had left them.[2]

Odessa Gittens, who began a teaching career after returning to Barbados, was typical of those who had served overseas. Her mind broadened by seeing the world, she was bright, ambitious and longing to shape the future of her island – a goal she had shared in meetings with a future Barbadian prime minister. It was such men and women who provided the new nations with their first generation of legislators and public servants. Yet, in the years after her return, Gittens faced open hostility and professional stagnation. Her perceived British mannerisms gave the impression she was putting on airs, and this provoked an unfortunate reaction.

> I was victimized, slandered and stigmatized, and everything was wrong with me. I had the worst period of my life in the first ten years after returning from England. Every woman ganged up against me, and I fought the battle and won. It was jealousy. I'd done nothing, but they had the jobs that I was recommended for by the Colonial Office.[3]

Even today, Barbadians returning home after successful and enriching careers in the United Kingdom or Canada complain that they are discriminated against by their island compatriots.

While the islands prepared for self-government and a redefinition of their relationship with the United Kingdom, a parallel and equally significant development was taking place. Many thousands of West Indians were in the process of emigrating to Britain, as well as to the United States and Canada. Those who had gone to work in the mother country during wartime had enjoyed a higher standard of living than was commonly attainable at home, and Britain's economy was now expanding. With its wartime losses and emigration of Britons to other parts of the world, the United Kingdom no longer had sufficient manpower to meet the demands of industry. British government agencies recruited workers in the Caribbean (the official status of these bodies enabled early West Indian migrants to boast that "the Queen invited us" to Britain); the first group of 492 travelled aboard the former troopship *Empire Windrush*, which docked at Tilbury on 21 June 1948.

This event is regarded as the beginning of multiracial Britain. Many of those who arrived then felt the same respect for the mother country that had prompted wartime volunteers (indeed, some immigrants were returning wartime servicemen), but they were to have a rude awakening. No longer seen by their hosts as allies in a common cause, they faced suspicion, discrimination and outright hostility. One of them, Connie Mark, remembered:

> I got very annoyed that people didn't want to accept how the West Indies were involved in the war and how we were brought up to love the King, love the Queen, to love England, and to respect England. Then when you come here after the war, what do you see? You see a sign saying "No Blacks, no Irish, no dogs, no children". That hurt, that really used to hurt.[4]

While jobs may have been plentiful in Britain, housing was not. Large groups of immigrants were considered a strain on resources that were already severely limited, and perhaps were thought to be taking amenities from those who were more entitled to them. Most West Indians could afford to live only in poorer areas; by congregating in particular districts – Notting Hill in west London was a well-known instance – they gave the impression of "taking over" parts of British cities. Most people in the United Kingdom had never previously met West Indians, while the British whom Caribbean people had encountered had been colonial administrators, soldiers and sailors. They had, therefore, visualized a nation of citizens that was far removed from their inner-city neighbours.

Any large group of new arrivals needs time to become accepted, and although signs reading "No Coloureds" were ubiquitous in major cities until 1970, blacks were not – as the quotation above makes clear – the only victims of discrimination. And not all discrimination was malicious. To successive commanding officers of British Army units despatched to British Guiana when the constitution was suspended in 1953, Whitehall's attitude to Anglo-Guianese marriages was consistently clear: they were to take all practicable measures to prevent such unions. To permit soldiers to return home with coloured wives would anger the parents of the young men – mostly immature conscripts away from home for the first time in their lives – who had married them. Furthermore, and this was a weighty factor in determining official policy, the Guianese girls – pretty, well educated, from relatively comfortable backgrounds and brought up in the climate and culture of that equatorial colony – had to be deterred from rashly entering into marriages that could condemn them to living in a slum in a depressed part of Britain.

Nevertheless, racial tension built up throughout the 1950s. It culminated in the summer of 1958 with a week of race riots in Notting Hill, in which white youths attacked blacks and destroyed property. The events were widely reported, and West Indians at home responded with outrage. Those who retained the traditional image of Britain were horrified that their friends and relations could be set upon in the capital city of the mother country. Both Bustamante and Manley visited England to reassure and commiserate with the victims, and there was some reciprocal anger against whites in the British Caribbean territories. To many West Indians the riots marked a parting of the ways between their own community and Britain, fuelling the desire for independence. There were, however, very few further outbreaks on this scale in the next half-century, and integration proved slow but successful. The arrival of *Empire Windrush* at Tilbury docks on 21 June 1948 was celebrated all over the United Kingdom as the beginning of a new era.

As the notion of federation gained currency during the 1950s, the question of defence was among the issues debated, and an important decision was reached: the WIR was to be revived as the Caribbean's single significant military unit. When the regiment had been stood down in 1927, one part of it – the band – had continued to exist. This body of musicians, highly distinctive in their colourful Zouave uniforms, proved a link between the colonial Caribbean and the new era of independent states. The recreated WIR would take on the traditions of not only the previous regular army regiments but also of the islands' local units. It would wear the old cap-badge and play the regimental march, and its officers would dine off the old mess silver. On 31 December 1958 Jamaica's volunteer unit assembled on parade and listened to a message from the governor, who said: "The West India Regiment will be established tomorrow and will absorb the greater part of the Jamaica Regiment. The Regiment will start with the priceless heritage of regimental tradition and efficiency which it will inherit from the former West India Regiment."[5]

But four years later the dream of federation ended, and with it the rebirth of the WIR. The territories set up their own individual defence forces, and in July 1962 the Jamaica Regiment was absorbed into the Jamaica Defence Force; other units such as the Barbados Regiment were likewise made part of the West Indies' disparate new security structures. Nevertheless, the merits of coordination in Caribbean defence matters have been recognized by the establishment of the Regional Security System (RSS) by Barbados and the Eastern Caribbean states.

The New Defence Force

Like the University of the West Indies, the Caribbean Court of Justice and the West Indies cricket team, the WIR was intended to promote a sense of common pride and shared heritage. It would be recruited from the various islands and would serve throughout the region – a means of introducing the troops to islands other than their own and building friendships between the Caribbean public and their soldiers.

In military terms the development was painless, for there was time to create a cadre of officers and NCOs trained and assisted by British personnel. Sir Kenneth Blackburn compared the islands favourably with postcolonial Africa when he wrote:

In East Africa there was hardly a single officer above the rank of subaltern in the whole of the African forces at the time of independence. It is hardly surprising that mutinies followed swiftly in the wake of home rule celebrations. No such problems arose in the West Indies. The Jamaica Regiment had West Indians as battalion and company commanders, with officers on loan from the British Army serving under them. The transition was smooth and easy in Jamaica, Trinidad, Barbados and British Guiana.[6]

The *Journal of the Trinidad and Tobago Regiment,* looking back on the period between federation and independence, provides a more detailed picture of the WIR and explains what happened to the unit once the collapse of the Federation had removed its *raison d'être*:

> For some time prior to September 1961, recruiting for the West India Regiment, which was the main fighting component of the Federal Defence Force, had been carried out on a federal basis. Men were recruited from all the islands of the Federation on a percentage basis related to the population of each territory. By September 20 1961 (the death-knell of the Federation) there were some 200 Trinidadian nationals serving in the Regiment.
>
> The Federal Government in dissolving the West India Regiment, allowed the men a number of choices; these can be summarized as follows:
>
> Nationals of Jamaica and Trinidad could either join their respective national defence forces or take a discharge.
>
> Nationals of the Leeward/Windward group and Barbados could join either the Trinidad or Jamaican Defence Forces, the British Army, or take a discharge.
>
> In the event, the results of the men's options showed that approximately 150 nationals of Trinidad and Tobago serving in the WIR wished to join their own territory's defence force and some 50 nationals of the "Little Eight" and Barbados were also accepted for transfer, thus making a total of about 200 trained soldiers available as a foundation on which to build any Trinidad and Tobago Defence Force.[7]

This publication goes on to describe how the regiment was set up. A large number of British officers and NCOs (in the officers' mess photograph, ten of the nineteen men are white) ensured that tradition was maintained:

> Our [regimental] birthday was Monday 23rd July, 1962. Of course a great deal had happened before then – the general plan had been drawn up, the establishment and equipment table had

been written, the uniform had been designed and some cooks had been recruited and had started training – but it was on that day that the NCOs of the old West India Regiment who lived in Trinidad reported for duty to St James' Barracks. They were quickly followed by those who lived in the Little Eight.[8]

Though independence soon came to the biggest islands – Jamaica and Trinidad and Tobago in August 1962 – the establishing of new nations was a surprisingly long process. Guyana and Barbados became independent in 1966, Grenada in 1974, St Lucia and St Vincent and the Grenadines in 1979, Antigua and Barbuda and Belize in 1981 and St Kitts and Nevis in 1983. A number of smaller islands – Montserrat, the Caymans, the Turks and Caicos, the British Virgin Islands and Anguilla – decided to remain British Dependent (now Overseas) Territories. In all cases a number of links with Britain remain – in overseas aid, defence agreements, education and training, law and policing or royal patronage.

The relationship today is dictated by both sentiment and practical needs. Unlike its erstwhile imperial rivals the French and the Dutch, Britain maintains no military garrisons in the Caribbean, but the Royal Navy provides a part-time "floating garrison" in the form of the Atlantic Patrol Task (North). The APT(N) warships provide useful assistance in the detection and arrest of drug-runners and in disaster relief. For the Caribbean people they are also a solitary reminder of a long and proud shared military and maritime history.

The West Indian nations and Britain are equal members of the Commonwealth and share the values of that unique worldwide institution. A special bond is still nurtured between all those who served in the armed forces and merchant navies of the British Empire and the Commonwealth. The region's ex-servicemen and servicewomen benefit from the charitable work of the Legion in each country, work generously sponsored by the Royal Canadian Legion under the umbrella of the Royal Commonwealth Ex-Services League. And on Remembrance Days throughout the West Indies, old comrades join with their fellow citizens in paying homage to those who gave their lives in conflicts past. But whether these traditional links with Britain will endure at the same level of intensity is debatable. Canada and the United States already have a greater influence on the life, opinions, economy and cultures of the Caribbean.

The Caribbean people have determined that their future lies in coming together in a common trading area. The Caribbean Community and Common Market (CARICOM) was established in 1973 and now consists of fifteen countries. In the face of globalization of world trade, the demise of traditional monocrops such as sugar and bananas, and the growth of alternative industries such as tourism and financial services, CARICOM members have agreed upon a Caribbean Single Market and Economy.

In Britain the West Indian community is making a conspicuous contribution to the nation – in Parliament, in the Health Service, on the stage, as writers, as athletes and, alas, as criminals too. As well, in the armed forces a young Grenadian soldier won the Victoria Cross while serving in Iraq (see appendix). Britain is now a multicultural society; its citizens of Asian and African parentage, people who belong in and identify with the United Kingdom, are a natural sequel to the surrender of empire. They continue a process that has marked its long history: influxes of Romans, Saxons, Normans, Huguenots, Jews and many others, all of whom created the nation, enriched its culture and brought with them a much needed labour force and skills. It is therefore only fitting that, after nearly four hundred years, the part played by West Indians in helping Britain and its empire to attain their unrivalled stature should at last be made known.

On independence that empire bequeathed to its former subjects many substantial gifts: a fully functioning Westminster system of government, relative prosperity with stable currencies and steadily rising standards of living; health care, clean water and social safety nets for the disadvantaged; and, most important of all, a high level of literacy. Their educational system, vastly improved since the pre-war Depression, equips West Indian men and women at last to compete on equal terms with their rivals in other lands in a world of advanced technology and global markets. This region, small but significant in the global world of achievement, has produced

no fewer than three Nobel laureates: Sir Arthur Lewis and Derek
Walcott from St Lucia, who won respectively prizes for economics
and literature, and Sir Vidiadhar (V.S.) Naipaul from Trinidad,
who won the prize for literature.

Since the time of Columbus, when our story opened five centuries ago, the people of the West Indies have come a long way.
Those living today have inherited a bounteous legacy. The challenge for the future is to build on that foundation, while never
forgetting the debt owed to those whose courage, staunchness and
sacrifice created that legacy.

Appendix A
The U-Boat War in the Caribbean: Some Facts

During the war the Germans built 1,162 U-boats; by March 1943 five new U-boats were coming into service each week. A total of 784 U-boats were lost on operations, and of the total strength of Admiral Karl Dönitz's U-boat arm of 40,200 sailors, some 31,000 lost their lives in battle. This arm suffered higher percentage losses than any other element of the German armed forces, but their pride never cracked and their morale remained superb to the end.

Table A.1: Top-Scoring U-Boat Commanders in the Caribbean Theatre

Commander	U-Boat	Tonnage Sunk	Ships Sunk/ Damaged
Adolf Piening	U-155	84,562	19/0
Jürgen Wattenburg	U-162	77,643	13/0
Hans Witt	U-129	76,184	16/0
Ernst Bauer	U-126	74,705	15/4
Georg Lassen	U-160	74,106	14/2
Günter Müller-Stockheim	U-67	72,731	11/5
Jürgen von Rosenstiel	U-502	71,272	13/1
Werner Hartenstein	U-156	67,529	16/7
Karl Merten	U-68	50,898	7/0
Georg Staats	U-508	50,195	11/0
Werner Henke	U-515	46,782	8/2

Commander	U-Boat	Tonnage Sunk	Ships Sunk/ Damaged
Erich Rostin	U-158	44,717	9/0
Harro Schacht	U-507	44,027	8/0
Richard Zapp	U-66	43,957	6/1
Friedrich Markworth	U-66	43,152	7/4
Helmut Witte	U-159	41,480	11/1
Albrecht Achilles	U-161	39,403	8/5

Source: Gaylord Kelshall, *The U-Boat War in the Caribbean* (Shrewsbury, UK: Airlife, 1994).

Appendix B
West Indians Awarded the Victoria Cross

Founded by Queen Victoria in 1856, this most highly esteemed decoration is conferred by the sovereign alone, upon advice, for the most conspicuous bravery or some daring pre-eminent act of valour or self-sacrifice or extreme devotion to duty in the presence of the enemy. Only 1,355 VCs have been awarded, many posthumously, since its founding.

Ambrose Madden, Sergeant, Forty-first (Welch) Regiment, later Lieutenant, Second West India Regiment; born Ireland 1820, died Jamaica 1863; for valour in the Crimea on 26 October 1854.

Henry Edward Jerome, Captain, Eighty-sixth (Irish) Regiment; born Antigua 1830, died Bath, England, 1901; for valour in India, at Jhansi on 3 April 1858 and at Jumna on 28 May in the same year.

Herbert Mackworth Clogstoun, Captain, Nineteenth (Madras) Native Infantry, Indian Army; born Port of Spain, Trinidad, 1820, died India 1862; for valour at Chichumbar, India, on 15 January 1859.

Samuel Hodge, Private, Fourth West India Regiment, born Tortola, Virgin Isles, 1840, died Belize 1868; for valour near River Gambia, West Africa, on 30 June 1866.

William St Lucien Chase, Lieutenant, Twenty-eighth Native Infantry, Indian Army; born St Lucia 1856, died Quetta, India, 1908; for valour near Kandahar, Afghanistan, on 16 August 1880.

William James Gordon, Lance-Corporal, West India Regiment; born Jamaica 1864, died Jamaica 1922; for valour in the Gambia, West Africa, on 13 March 1892.

Johnson Beharry, Private, The Princess of Wales's Royal Regiment; born Grenada 1979; for valour in Maysan province, Iraq, in May and June 2004.

Three men have won the VC twice (VC and Bar):

Arthur Martin-Leake, born Ware, Hertfordshire, England, 1874, died there 1953; for valour first as Surgeon-Captain in the South African Constabulary at Vlakfontein, South Africa, on 8 February 1902, and second as Lieutenant-Colonel, Royal Army Medical Corps, near Zonnebeke, Belgium, 31 July to 2 August 1917.

Noel Godfrey Chavasse, Captain, Royal Army Medical Corps; born Oxford, England, 1884, died Belgium 4 August 1917; for valour first at Guillemont, France, on 9 August 1916, and second at Wieltje, Belgium, 31 July to 2 August 1917.

Charles Hazlitt Upham, Twentieth Battalion (Canterbury Regiment), New Zealand Expeditionary Force; born Christchurch, New Zealand, 1908; for valour first as a Second Lieutenant in Crete, 22 to 30 May 1941, and second as a Captain at El Ruweisat Ridge, Western Desert, Egypt, 14/15 July 1942.

Appendix C
Private Johnson Gideon Beharry Receives the Victoria Cross

A spring day in London. Outside Buckingham Palace the crush of spectators and photographers suggested that more was going on than the usual Changing of the Guard. It was an investiture, and there was a considerable flurry of interest as the recipients emerged after the ceremony.

One of them was the yachtswoman Ellen Macarthur. In a tradition going back to Francis Drake and Francis Chichester, she had been honoured for sailing around the world – alone, and in record time. Though this was clearly for her a moment of personal glory, she told reporters that she felt "pretty humble". She, after all, had chosen to do what she did. The young men in khaki uniforms standing a few feet away had had no choice.

She was referring to several members of the 1st Battalion, Princess of Wales's Royal Regiment, who had just been decorated for bravery. They too were a source of public fascination, for their unit had won more gallantry awards than any other single unit in a single campaign since the Second World War. The tally included a Queen's Commendation and no fewer than fifteen mentions in despatches. There were two MBEs, two Conspicuous Gallantry Crosses, seven Military Crosses, two DSOs – and a Victoria Cross.

The recipient of the VC was the real star of the show. He was Private Johnson Beharry, a tall, handsome young man from Grenada. As the driver of a Warrior armoured personnel carrier, his quick thinking, professionalism and consistent courage had saved his vehicle and all its crew when it ran into an ambush. He had suffered wounds, and had the scars to prove it, but he smiled pleasantly for the cameras. When asked about his reaction to the ambush, he had modestly put his success down to teamwork and training. He had known, he said, that he had to get everyone out, because he couldn't have lived with himself otherwise. He sounded the archetypal military hero.

Others added their comments. Private Beharry's uncle, the hurricane that had hit his home island only ten months earlier still fresh in his memory, felt that the whole population would share his pride in his nephew's achievement and that this would help their morale and their recovery. "This is a great thing for Grenada," he said. Also present was General Sir Mike Jackson, the chief of the General Staff. The *Times* (28 April 2005, 7) quoted his professional assessment: "The utter selflessness of saving the other members of his team says everything about him. He is a wonderful embodiment of the fighting spirit of the British Army, and he would make a great recruiter."

This flattering tribute from such a senior officer was, in a sense, a vindication for all the men from the Caribbean region who served Britain with skill and courage, in such a wide range of units and campaigns and theatres of war, for more than two centuries.

Official Citation of Private Johnson Gideon Beharry, VC

Private Beharry carried out two individual acts of great heroism by which he saved the lives of his comrades. Both were in direct face of the enemy, under intense fire, at great personal risk to himself (one leading to him sustaining very serious injuries). His valour is worthy of the highest recognition.

In the early hours of the 1st May 2004 Beharry's company was ordered to replenish an isolated Coalition Forces outpost located in the centre of the troubled city of Al Amarah. He was the driver of a platoon commander's Warrior armoured fighting vehicle. His platoon was the company's reserve force and was placed on immediate notice to move. As the main elements of his company were moving into the city to carry out the replenishment, they were re-tasked to fight through a series of enemy ambushes in order to extract a foot patrol that had become pinned down under sustained small arms and heavy machine gun fire and improvised explosive device and rocket-propelled grenade attack.

Beharry's platoon was tasked over the radio to come to the assistance of the remainder of the company, who were attempting to extract the isolated foot patrol. As his platoon passed a roundabout, en route to the pinned-down patrol, they became aware that the road to the front was empty of all civilians and traffic – an indicator of a potential ambush ahead. The platoon commander ordered the vehicle to halt, so that he could assess the situation. The vehicle was then immediately hit by multiple rocket-propelled grenades. Eyewitnesses report that the vehicle was engulfed in a number of violent explosions, which physically rocked the 30-tonne Warrior. As a result of this ferocious initial volley of fire, both the platoon commander and the vehicle's gunner was incapacitated by concussion and óther wounds, and a number of the soldiers in the rear of the vehicle were also wounded. Due to damage sustained in the blast to the vehicle's radio systems, Beharry had no means of communication with either his turret crew or any of the other Warrior vehicles deployed around him. He did not know if his commander or crewmen were still alive, or how serious their injuries may be. In this confusing and dangerous situation, on his own initiative, he closed his driver's hatch and moved forward through the ambush position to try to establish some form of communications, halting just short of a barricade placed across the road.

The vehicle was hit again by sustained rocket-propelled grenade attack from insurgent fighters in the alleyways and on rooftops around his vehicle. Further damage to the Warrior from these explosions caused it to catch fire and fill rapidly with thick, noxious smoke. Beharry opened up his armoured hatch cover to clear his view and orientate himself to the situation. He still had no radio communications and was now acting on his own initiative, as the lead vehicle of a six Warrior convoy in an enemy-controlled area of the city at night. He assessed that his best course of action to save the lives of his crew was to push through, out of the ambush. He drove his Warrior directly through the barricade, not knowing if there were mines or improvised explosive devices placed there to destroy his vehicle. By doing this he was able to lead the remaining five Warriors behind him towards safety.

As the smoke in his driver's tunnel cleared, he was just able to make out the shape of another rocket-propelled grenade in flight heading directly towards him. He pulled the heavy armoured hatch down with one hand, whilst still controlling his vehicle with the other. However, the overpressure from the explosion of the rocket wrenched the hatch out of his grip, and the flames and force of the blast passed directly over him, down the driver's tunnel, further wounding the semi-conscious gunner in the turret. The impact of this rocket destroyed Beharry's armoured periscope, so he was forced to drive the vehicle through the remainder of the ambushed route, some 1500 metres long, with his hatch opened up and his head exposed to enemy fire, all the time with no communications with any other vehicle. During this long surge through the ambushes the vehicle was again struck by rocket-propelled grenades and small arms fire. While his head remained out of the hatch, to enable him to see the route ahead, he was directly exposed to much of this fire, and was himself hit by a 7.62mm bullet, which penetrated his helmet and remained lodged on its inner surface.

Despite this harrowing weight of incoming fire Beharry continued to push through the extended ambush, still leading his platoon until he broke down. He then visually identified another Warrior from his company and followed it through the streets of Al Amarah to the outside of the Cimic House outpost, which was receiving small arms fire from the surrounding area. Once he had brought his vehicle to a halt outside, without thought for his own personal safety, he climbed onto the turret of the still-burning vehicle and, seemingly oblivious to the incoming enemy small arms fire, man-handled his wounded platoon commander out of the turret, off the vehicle and to the safety of a nearby Warrior. He then returned once again to his vehicle and again mounted the exposed turret to lift out the vehicle's gunner and move him to a position of safety. Exposing himself yet again to enemy fire he returned to the rear of the burning vehicle to lead the disorientated and shocked dismounts and casualties to safety. Remounting his burning vehicle for the third time, he drove it through a complex chicane and into the security of the defended perimeter of the outpost, thus denying it to the enemy. Only at this stage did Beharry pull the fire extinguisher handlers, immobilizing the engine of the vehicle, dismounted and then moved himself into the relative safety of the back of another Warrior. Once inside Beharry collapsed from the sheer physical and mental exhaustion of his efforts and was subsequently himself evacuated.

Having returned to duty following medical treatment, on the 11th June 2004 Beharry's Warrior was part of a quick reaction force tasked to attempt to cut off a mortar team that had attacked a Coalition Force base in Al Amarah. As the lead vehicle of the platoon he was moving rapidly through the dark city streets towards the suspected firing point, when his vehicle was ambushed by the enemy from a series of rooftop positions. During this initial heavy weight of enemy fire, a rocket-propelled grenade detonated on the vehicle's frontal armour, just six inches from Beharry's head, resulting in a serious head injury. Other rockets struck the turret and sides of the vehicle, incapacitating his commander and injuring several of the crew. With the blood from his head injury obscuring his vision, Beharry managed to continue to control his vehicle, and forcefully reversed the Warrior out of the ambush area. The vehicle continued to move until it struck the wall of a nearby building and came to rest. Beharry then lost consciousness as a result of his wounds. By moving the vehicle out of the enemy's chosen killing area he enabled other Warrior crews to be able to extract his crew from his vehicle, with a greatly reduced risk from incoming fire. Despite receiving a serious head injury, which later saw him being listed as very seriously injured and in a coma for some time, his level-headed actions in the face of heavy and accurate enemy fire at short range again almost certainly saved the lives of his crew and provided the conditions for their safe evacuation to medical treatment.

Beharry displayed repeated extreme gallantry and unquestioned valour, despite intense direct attacks, personal injury and damage to his vehicle in the face of relentless enemy action.

Notes

Chapter 1

1. G.E. Bourne, ed., *The Northmen, Columbus and Cabot 985–1503* (New York: Scribner's, 1906), 77–80.

2. Gianni Granzotto, *Christopher Columbus* (London: Collins, 1986), 282–83. The late Charles Goff, professor emeritus, Yale School of Medicine, developed the gunshot theory.

Chapter 2

1. I.A. Wright, *Spanish Documents Concerning English Voyages in the Caribbean, 1527–1568* (London: Hakluyt Society, 1932), quoted in Sir Alan Burns, *History of the West Indies* (London: Allen and Unwin, 1965), 141.

Chapter 3

1. Eliot Warburton, *Memoirs of Prince Rupert and the Cavaliers* (London: Richard Bentley, 1849), 375–77.

Chapter 5

1. Channel 4, "Black and Asian History Map", http://www.channel4.com/history/microsites/B/blackhistorymap/

2. Pedro Welch, "Practice and Malpractice: British Military Doctors and Their Patients in the Eighteenth and Nineteenth Century Caribbean", *Journal of the Barbados Museum and Historical Society* 51 (December 2005): 128.

3. Brian Dyde, *The Empty Sleeve: The Story of the West India Regiments of the British Army* (St John's, Antigua: Hansib Caribbean, 1997), 72.

Chapter 6

1. *Calendar of State Papers, 1696–97, America and West Indies,* quoted in Burns, *History of the West Indies,* 279.

2. Burns, *History of the West Indies,* 315.

3. Ibid., 446.

4. Roger Buckley, *Slaves in Red Coats* (New Haven: Yale University Press, 1979), 2.

5. *Annual Register, 1781,* quoted in Burns, *History of the West Indies,* 526.

Chapter 7

1. Mary Seacole, *The Wonderful Adventures of Mrs Seacole in Many Lands* (reprint, Bristol, UK: Falling Wall Press, 1984), 193.

Chapter 8

1. Lieutenant F.J. Davies, quoted in Dyde, *Empty Sleeve,* 24.

Chapter 9

1. *Federalist* (Barbados), in undated clippings assembled by the Islington Borough Library Service, London, for Black History Month.

2. *West Indian* (Grenada), in undated clippings assembled by the Islington Borough Library Service, London, for Black History Month.

3. *London Gazette,* in undated clippings assembled by the Islington Borough Library Service, London, for Black History Month.

4. *Stratford Express* (London), in undated clippings assembled by the Islington Borough Library Service, London, for Black History Month.

5. Frank Cundall, *Jamaica's Part in the Great War, 1914–1918* (London: West India Committee on behalf of the Institute of Jamaica, 1925), 39.

6. Ibid., 45.

7. Ibid., 56.

8. Ibid., 57.

9. Ibid., 75.

Chapter 10

1. E. Smith, typescript, Department of Documents, Imperial War Museum, 461.
2. Ibid.

Chapter 11

1. Grenada National Museum, *Grenada in World War II* (St Georges: Grenada National Museum, n.d.), 1.
2. North Kensington Archives, *The Caribbean at War* (London: North Kensington Archives, 1992), 3.
3. Authors' collection of notes and comments from West Indians on the Second World War and other conflicts.
4. Ibid.
5. Ephemera Collection, K14179, Department of Printed Books, Imperial War Museum.
6. Interview with the authors and Claire Collinson-Jones, Insight TV, *War in the Caribbean* (typescript, 2004).
7. Ephemera Collection, K11906.
8. Jill Hamilton, "Memories of Jill Hamilton's Experiences During World War II" (typescript, 1 April 2002, private archive).
9. Ephemera Collection, K90511.
10. Ephemera Collection, K14535.
11. Squadron Leader Ulric Cross, DSO, DFC, telephone interview by the authors, 2005.
12. North Kensington Archives, *Caribbean at War*, 21.
13. T.J. Finlayson, *The Fortress Came First* (Gibraltar: Gibraltar Books, 1991), 57–58.
14. "One of the evacuees", 18 January 1941, quoted ibid., 82.
15. Editorial, *Daily Gleaner,* early November 1940, quoted in Finlayson, *Fortress,* 77–78.
16. *Jamaica Times,* 23 November 1940, quoted in Finlayson, *Fortress,* 79.
17. Helen Follett, *Islands on Guard* (New York: Scribner's, 1943), 63.
18. Ibid.

Chapter 12

1. Athelstan Holden, interview with the authors and Claire Collinson-Jones, Insight TV, *War in the Caribbean* (typescript, 2004).

2. Interview with the authors and Claire Collinson-Jones, Insight TV, *War in the Caribbean* (typescript, 2004).

3. George M. Topping, "Wild Dogs or Ambassadors" (unpublished manuscript, n.d.). Subsequent quotes in this section are from this work, unless otherwise indicated.

4. Misc. papers, Department of Printed Books, Imperial War Museum.

5. Topping, "Wild Dogs".

6. Amos Ford, *Telling the Truth: The Life and Times of the British Honduran Forestry Unit in Scotland (1941–44)* (London: Karia Press, 1985), 6.

7. Ibid., 67.

8. Ibid., 74.

9. Marika Sherwood, *The British Honduran Forestry Unit in Scotland, 1941–44* (London: Karia Press, 1985), iv.

10. Ben Bousquet and Colin Douglas, *West Indian Women at War* (London: Lawrence and Wishart, 1991), 86

11. Ibid.

12. *Hulton's National Weekly* 21, no. 10 (4 December 1943).

13. Margaret Clairmonte, interview with the authors and Claire Collinson-Jones, Insight TV, *War in the Caribbean* (typescript, 2004).

14. Cynthia Boyd, interview with the authors and Claire Collinson-Jones, Insight TV, *War in the Caribbean* (typescript, 2004).

15. Clairmonte, interview.

16. Ibid.

17. Boyd, interview.

18. Clairmonte, interview.

19. Misc. newspaper files, Department of Printed Books, Imperial War Museum.

20. George Powe, quoted in Anon., "The Commonwealth at War" (lecture notes, Islington Borough Library Service, Black History Month, October 2004), 14.

21. Gerald Beard, quoted ibid.

22. Julian Marryshow, personal communication, n.d.

23. Ex-serviceman #7123 Private Michael Smith (typescript, n.d., private archive).

24. A.E. Stokes-Roberts, "The West Indian Forces", *Barbados Advocate,* 16 August 1944, 7.

25. Ibid.

26. Interview with the authors and Claire Collinson-Jones, Insight TV, *War in the Caribbean* (typescript, 2004).

27. Harold Macmillan, quoted in Anon., "Commonwealth at War", 28.

Chapter 13

1. Reginald Gooding, "The Day World War II Came to the Caribbean", *Bajan,* August 1978.

Chapter 14

1. UK Ministry of Defence (Navy), *German Naval History: The U-Boat War* (London: Her Majesty's Stationery Office, 1989), 39.

2. Ibid., 17–20.

3. Lawrence Paterson, *U-Boat War Patrol* (London: Greenhill Books, 2004), 135–38.

Chapter 15

1. Lieutenant Commander E.E. Barringer (RNVR), typescript, 91/17/1 (Department of Documents, Imperial War Museum).

2. Ministry of Defence, *German Naval History,* 14.

3. S. France, typescript, 82/27/1 (Department of Documents, Imperial War Museum).

4. Topping, "Wild Dogs", 8.

5. J. Lisle, typescript, 80/18/1 (Department of Documents, Imperial War Museum).

6. Ibid.

7. "West Indian Merchant Seaman", typescript (Department of Documents, Imperial War Museum).

8. J. St Hill Jones (ex-serviceman, Merchant Navy), typescript (private archive, n.d.).

9. Topping, "Wild Dogs", 8.

10. Captain E. Monkton, typescript, 85/29/1 (Department of Documents, Imperial War Museum).

11. France, typescript.

12. Ford, *Telling the Truth*, 37.

13. Monkton, typescript.

14. *Barbados Advocate*, 28 April 1942.

15. Monkton, typescript.

16. *Barbados Advocate*, 28 April 1942.

17. Monkton, typescript.

18. Paterson, *U-Boat War Patrol*, 167–69.

19. Monkton, typescript.

20. Gaylord Kelshall, *The U-Boat War in the Caribbean* (Shrewsbury, UK: Airlife, 1994), 440.

Chapter 16

1. Sir Kenneth Blackburn, *Lasting Legacy: A Story of British Colonialism* (London: Johnson Publications, 1976), 196–67.

2. Bousquet and Douglas, *West Indian Women*, 145.

3. Ibid., 146.

4. Stephen Bourne and Sav Kyriacou, eds., *A Ship and a Prayer* (London: Borough of Hammersmith and Fulham, 1999), 24.

5. West India Regiment, http://www.regiments.org/regiments/westindies/regts/wi-wir.htm.

6. Blackburn, *Lasting Legacy*, 194–95.

7. Lieutenant-Colonel B.J. Eastwood, "Early Days", *Journal of the Trinidad and Tobago Regiment* 1, no. 1 (December 1962): 5.

8. Ibid.

Bibliography

Books

Alleyne, Warren. *Barbados at War, 1939–45.* Barbados: Warren Alleyne, 1999.

Anon. *Sketches and Recollections of the West Indies by a Resident.* London: Smith, Elder, 1828.

Baptiste, Fitzroy André. *The European Possessions in the Caribbean in World War II: Dimensions of Great Power Co-operation and Conflict.* New York: Greenwood Press, 1983

———. *War, Co-operation and Conflict: The European Possessions in the Caribbean, 1939–1945.* New York: Greenwood Press, 1988.

Blackburn, Kenneth. *Lasting Legacy: A Story of British Colonialism.* London: Johnson Publications, 1976.

Blair, Clay. *Hitler's U-Boat War: The Hunters, 1939–1942.* London: Weidenfeld and Nicholson, 1997.

Bourne, G.E. ed. *The Northmen, Columbus and Cabot 985–1503.* New York: Scribner's, 1906.

Bourne, Stephen, and Sav Kyriacou, eds. *A Ship and a Prayer.* London: Borough of Hammersmith and Fulham, 1999.

Bousquet, Ben, and Colin Douglas. *West Indian Women at War.* London: Lawrence and Wishart, 1991.

Buckley, Roger N. *The British Army in the West Indies.* Kingston: University of the West Indies Press, 1998.

———. *Slaves in Red Coats.* New Haven: Yale University Press, 1979.

Burns, Alan. *History of the West Indies.* London: Allen and Unwin, 1965.

Campbell, P.F. *An Outline of Barbados History.* Bridgetown: Caribbean Graphics, 1974.

Carnegie, James, and Patricia Patterson. *The People Who Came,* vol. 2. Edinburgh: Pearson Educational, 1989.

Chartrand, Rene, and Paul Chappell. *British Forces in the West Indies, 1793–1815.* London: Osprey, 1996.

Cundall, Frank. *Jamaica's Part in the Great War, 1914–1918.* London: West India Committee on behalf of Institute of Jamaica, 1925.

Dachner, Dan, and Dene Dachner. *A Traveler's Guide to Caribbean History.* Dixon, Calif.: Traveler's Press, 1997.

Dilkes, David. *Great Britain, the Commonwealth and the Wider World, 1939–45.* University of Hull Press, 1998.

Dyde, Brian. *The Empty Sleeve: The Story of the West India Regiments of the British Army.* St John's, Antigua: Hansib Caribbean, 1997.

Ellis, A.B. *The History of the First West India Regiment.* London: Chapman and Hall, 1885.

Finlayson, T.J. *The Fortress Came First.* Gibraltar: Gibraltar Books, 1991.

Follett, Helen. *Islands on Guard.* New York: Charles Scribner's Sons, 1943.

Ford, Amos A. *Telling the Truth: The Life and Times of the British Honduran Forestry Unit in Scotland (1941–44).* London: Karia Press, 1985.

Fortescue, J.W. *A History of the British Army.* London: Macmillan, 1912.

Graham. John. *Ponder Anew: Reflections on the Twentieth Century.* Kent, UK: Spellmount, 1999.

Granzotto, Gianni. *Christopher Columbus.* London: Collins, 1986.

Guy, Alan, ed. *The Road to Waterloo.* London: National Army Museum/Alan Sutton, 1990.

Halliday, Andrew. *The West Indies.* London: John William Parker, 1837.

Hamshere, Cyril. *The British in the Caribbean.* Cambridge, MA: Harvard University Press, 1972.

Honychurch, Lennox. *The Caribbean People,* vol. 2. London: Thomas Nelson and Sons, 1980.

Howe, Glenford. *Race, War and Nationalism: A Social History of West Indians in the First World War.* Kingston: Ian Randle, 2002.

Imperial War Museum. *Together: The Contribution Made in the Second World War by African, Asian and Caribbean Men and Women.* London: Imperial War Museum, 1994.

James, Lawrence. *The Rise and Fall of the British Empire*. London: Little, Brown, 1994.

Kelshall, Gaylord M. *The U-Boat War in the Caribbean*. Shrewsbury, UK: Airlife, 1994.

Kleinman, Joseph, and Eileen Kurtis-Kleinman. *Life on an African Slave Ship*. San Diego: Lucent Books, 2000.

Kostam, A., and J.M. Showell. *Seventh U-Boat Flotilla*. Hersham, UK: Ian Allan, 2003.

Mitchell, Harold. *Europe in the Caribbean*. Stanford University Press/Hispanic American Society, 1963.

Murray, Robert. *Lest We Forget: The Experiences of World War II West Indian Ex-Service Personnel*. St John's, Antigua: Hansib Caribbean, 1996.

North Kensington Archives. *The Caribbean at War*. London: North Kensington Archives, 1992.

Palmer, Alan, ed. *Dictionary of the British Empire and Commonwealth*. London: John Murray, 1996.

Paterson, Lawrence. *U-Boat War Patrol*. London: Greenhill Books, 2004.

Pocock, Tom. *Horatio Nelson*, London: Pimlico, 1994.

Register of the Victoria Cross. Cheltenham: This England, 1981.

Schama, Simon. *A History of Britain*. Vol. 3, *1776–2000*. London: BBC Worldwide, 2002.

Seacole, Mary. *The Wonderful Adventures of Mrs Seacole in Many Lands*. Reprint, Bristol, UK: Falling Wall Press, 1984.

Sherwood, Marika. *The British Honduran Forestry Unit in Scotland, 1941–44*. London: Karia Press, 1985.

Smith, Victor T.C. *Fire and Brimstone*. Basseterre, St Kitts: Creole Publishing, 1992.

Trollope, Anthony. *The West Indies and the Spanish Main*. London: Chapman and Hall, 1860.

United Kingdom Ministry of Defence (Navy). *German Naval History: The U-Boat War in the Atlantic*. London: Her Majesty's Stationery Office, 1989.

Warburton, Eliot. *Memoirs of Prince Rupert and the Cavaliers*. London: Richard Bentley, 1849.

Williams, Eric. *Documents of West Indian History, 1492–1655*. Port of Spain: PNM Publishing, 1963.

———. *From Columbus to Castro: The History of the Caribbean*. New York: Vintage Books, 1970.

Articles

"Americans in the Caribbean". *National Geographic,* June 1942.

Eastwood, B.J. "Early Days". *Journal of the Trinidad and Tobago Regiment* 1, no. 1 (December 1962).

"The Girl from the West Indies". *Hulton's National Weekly* 21, no. 10 (4 December 1943): 2–6.

Gooding, Reginald. "The Day World War II Came to the Caribbean". *Bajan,* August 1978.

Hamilton, Alan. "Queen Honours a Modest, but Living, Testament to Courage". *Times* (London), 28 April 2005.

Hardman, Robert. "You're Very Special". *Daily Mail,* 28 April 2005.

Low, Valentine. "My Hero". *Evening Standard* (London), 27 April 2005.

Stokes-Roberts, A.E. "The West Indian Forces". *Barbados Advocate,* 16 August 1944.

Welch, Pedro. "Practice and Malpractice: British Military Doctors and Their Patients in the Eighteenth and Nineteenth Century Caribbean". *Journal of the Barbados Museum and Historical Society* 51 (December 2005).

Unpublished Sources

Barringer, E.E. Typescript 91/17/1. Department of Documents, Imperial War Museum.

France, S. Typescript 82/27/1. Department of Documents, Imperial War Museum.

Hamilton, Jill. "Memories of Jill Hamilton's Experiences During World War II". Typescript, 1 April 2002. Private archive.

Imperial War Museum, Department of Printed Books. Ephemera Collection: K11905, K14179, K14472, K14535, K15651.

Jones, J. St Hill. Typescript, n.d. Private archive.

Lisle, J. Typescript 80/18/1. Department of Documents, Imperial War Museum.

Monkton, E. Typescript 85/29/1. Department of Documents, Imperial War Museum.

Morgan, P. Typescript, n.d. Private archive.

Owen, L.O. Typescript 83/4/1. Department of Documents, Imperial War Museum.

Owen, P.J. (Intelligence Corps). "Defence of Orange Walk". Typescript.

Smith, E. Typescript. Department of Documents, Imperial War Museum.

Smith, Michael. Typescript, n.d. Private archive.

Topping, George M. "Wild Dogs or Ambassadors". Manuscript, n.d. Private archive.

"West Indian Merchant Seamen". Typescript. Department of Documents, Imperial War Museum.

Index